UNIFORMS, DISTINCTION AND OTHER INSIGNIA OF THE AUSTRO-HUNGARIAN ARMY 1877-1897

FROM OLD COLLECTOR'S BOOKS,
WITH REVISED AND RESTORED PLATES
BY RUHL, KULAS, FRANCESCHINI
AND OTHER ARTISTS

SOLDIERSHOP PUBLISHING

NOTE ABOUT BOOK PRINTING BEFORE 1930

This book may contain text or images coming from a reproduction of a book published before 1930 (over seventy years ago). No effort has been made to modernize or standardize the spelling used in the original text, so this book may have occasional imperfections such as missing or blurred pages, poor pictures, errant marks, etc. that were either part of the original artifact, or were introduced by the scanning process. We believe this work is culturally important, and despite the imperfections, have elected to bring it back into print (digital and/or paper) as part of our continuing commitment to the preservation of printed works worldwide. We appreciate your understanding of the imperfections in the preservation process, and hope you enjoy this valuable book. Now this book is purpose re-built and is proof-read and re-type set from the original to provide an outstanding experience of reflowing text, also for an ebook reader. However Soldiershop publishing added, enriched, revised and overhauled the text, images, etc. of the cover and the book. Therefore, the job is now to all intents and purposes a derivative work, and the added, new and original parts of the book are the copyright of Soldiershop. On this second unpublished part of the book none of images or text may be reproduced in any format without the expressed written permission of Soldiershop. Almost many of the images of our books and prints are taken from original first edition prints or books that are no longer in copyright and are therefore public domain. We have been a specialized bookstore for a long time so we (and several friends antiquarian booksellers) have readily available a lot of ancient, historical and illustrated books not in copyright. Each of our prints, art designs or illustrations is either our own creation, or a fully digitally restoration by our computer artists, or non copyrighted images. All of our prints are "tagged" with a registered digital copyright. Soldiershop remains to disposition of the possible having right for all the doubtful sources images or not identifies.

LICENSES COMMONS

Much of the Text And images in this book are from the *"Tipi militari dei differenti corpi che compomgono il Reale esercito e l'Armata di mare del Regno delle due Sicilie per Antonio Zezon. Napoli 1850"* of the Vinkhuijzen Collection now in the property of NYPL, library that we sincerely thank for granting permission to publish. This book may utilize material marked with license creative commons 3.0 or 4.0 (CC BY 4.0), (CC BY-ND 4.0), (CC BY-SA 4.0) or (CC0 1.0). We give appropriate attribution credit and indicate if change were made below in the acknowledgements field.

Title: **UNIFORMS, DISTINCTION AND OTHER INSIGNIA OF THE AUSTRO-HUNGARIAN ARMY 1877-1897 (SWU-800-026)**

Edited by Luca Stefano Cristini. Series edit for the brand *Soldiershop*.

First edition May 2025. Cover & Art Design: Luca S. Cristini. ISBN code: 979-12-5589-2403

Published by Luca Cristini Editore, via Orio 33/D- 24050 Zanica (BG) ITALY. www.soldiershop.com

UNIFORMS, DISTINCTION AND OTHER INSIGNIA OF THE AUSTRO-HUNGARIAN ARMY 1877-1897

FROM OLD COLLECTOR'S BOOKS, WITH REVISED AND RESTORED PLATES BY RUHL, KULAS, FRANCESCHINI AND OTHER ARTISTS

EDITED BY LUCA STEFANO CRISTINI

BERGAMO (ITALY) 2025

▲ Portrait of Kaiser Franz Joseph in 1873. by Franz von Lenbach. Kunsthistorisches Museum Vienna Austria.

Military Uniforms and Equipment of the Austro-Hungarian Army (1875–1900)

For the first time ever, the renowned treatise on the uniforms of the Imperial and Royal (K.u.K.) Austro-Hungarian Army from the 1880s—originally published by Moritz Rühl in Leipzig—is now available in an English translation.

This edition not only presents the complete text in English but also features meticulously restored color plates, ensuring the finest possible graphic reproduction. Additionally, the appendix includes a selection of exquisite and historically valuable plates from the same era, painted by J. V. Kulas, F. Franceschini, as well as Rühl's supplementary text *"Die österreichisch-ungarische Armee"* (pre-1881/82). These sources, drawn from the fully restored plates of the Viskuezzen Collection, offer a fascinating glimpse into the uniforms and organization of the Imperial Army.

THE K.U.K. ARMY IN THE YEARS FROM 1880-1890

Between 1875 and 1900, the Austro-Hungarian military uniforms underwent significant changes, reflecting both functional needs and political shifts. The uniforms of the German and Hungarian troops, the Landwehr, the Navy, as well as the Georgian-Bosnian and Tyrolean regiments, evolved in response to warfare advancements and national identity.

Uniform Reforms and Symbolism

In 1849–50, the Austro-Hungarian army adopted a double coat of arms, which was simplified to a single version in 1859. From that year onward, officers wore their sashes over the right shoulder, but by 1868, the sash was returned to its traditional placement around the waist, paired with gray trousers.

The Shift from White to Gray

The traditional white uniforms of the Imperial army proved impractical during the German unification wars (1864 and 1866), as advances in firearms made soldiers in bright colors easy targets. This led to a gradual move toward more subdued tones, culminating in the official adoption of the standard gray military uniform in 1909.

Equipment Modernization

In 1868, the army introduced new black leather gear—including belts, cartridge holders, and bags—for male soldiers. However, by 1881, these were replaced with brown leather equipment under the new "1881 pattern."

The "k.u.k. Army" and Its Final Designation

The Austro-Hungarian military was commonly referred to as the "k.u.k. Army" (Kaiserlich und königlich, meaning "Imperial and Royal"). This title was formally adopted in 1889, solidifying the dual monarchy's military identity.

▲ Portrait of an Austrian dragoon 1900. Painted by Ludwig Koch

THE UNIFORMS DISTINCTIVE AND OTHER INSIGNIA OF THE AUSTRO-HUNGARIAN IMPERIAL ARMY

1ST PART FROM THE AUSTRIAN BOOK: UNIFORMEN UND ABZEICHEN DER ÖSTERR.-UNGAR. WEHRMACHT BY K. K. COLONEL M. JUDEX. LEIPZIG 1880-1908, PUBLISHED BY MORITZ RUHL

GENERAL INFORMATION

Although the color illustrations and their accompanying explanations are sufficient to provide an overview of the uniforms of the entire armed forces, textual clarifications may still be useful for better understanding—particularly for military instruction—to ensure that this work covers all relevant information. Therefore, a detailed description is provided, with the following general remarks:

-Headgear

Headgear is divided into **parade** and **ordinary** headgear.

Parade headgear includes:

- Hat (*Hut*)
- Busby (*Kalpak*)
- Helmet (*Helm*)
- Shako (*Czako*)
- Lancers' cap (*Czapka*)
- Cap (*Kappe*), etc.

These are worn only in peacetime for **gala events, parades**, and other appropriate occasions. However, **cavalry and horse artillery** also wear them for **marching order** and **in the field**.

Ordinary headgear consists of the **officers' and enlisted field cap**, worn in peacetime for **daily service and off-duty wear**. In the field (except for cavalry and horse artillery), it is the **only headgear** used.

-Uniform Jackets

The **Waffenrock (tunic), Attila (hussar jacket), and Uhlanka (lancer jacket)** are **parade uniforms** for peacetime and are also worn off-duty when regulations or etiquette require.

In the **field** and for **marching order**, only **cavalry and horse artillery** wear them.

In **warm weather**, cavalry drape the **fur coat (*Pelz*)** over the tunic.

The number of button rows (one or two) on the front of these garments is clearly indicated in the color illustrations and further explained in the text. It should also be noted that the **tunics of officers** and **cadet officer deputies** (not assigned to any pay grade)

-Additional Notes on Uniforms

It should also be mentioned that the **tunics (Waffenröcke)** of **officers, cadet officer deputies, non-commissioned officers not assigned to a pay grade**, and **cadets in military academies** have **six buttons** on the rear pocket flaps, whereas **enlisted tunics** have only **two waist buttons** in this area—**except for Uhlans (lancers)**, who also have six buttons.

Fur-lined jackets (Pelzröcke, Uhlanka, winter Attila) are **only prescribed for mounted troops**. However, officers of other branches may wear **fur-lined tunics** in winter.

-Trousers

Trousers, designated under various names—such as **Pantalon, Salonhose (dress trousers), Stiefelhose (riding breeches), Tuchhose (cloth trousers)**, etc.—are described in detail below.

Pantalon (formal dress trousers) are worn **exclusively by generals** for gala occasions; otherwise, they are a standard uniform item.

Salonhose (recently called "blue-gray Pantalon with piping") are worn **only off-duty and for certain service duties** by officers and officer deputies of troops who wear **riding breeches and high boots** (e.g., cavalry, artillery, train troops). They have now also been adopted by officers of other branches and are permitted for **cadets and long-serving NCOs** of certain units when off-duty.

Stiefelhose (riding breeches) are worn—in addition to the mounted troops specified elsewhere—by **mounted officers of infantry units** (similar to their prescribed Pantalon), paired with **high boots and spurs**.

- **Field-gray or buckskin riding breeches without piping** are worn by all mounted officers for **regular duty** (except parades).
- In the **field and for marching order**, they are also worn by:
  - Aides-de-camp (*Flügeladjutanten*)
  - Officers of the **General Staff** and **Engineer Corps**
  - **Medical troops**
  - For marching order, officers of:
    - **Rifle troops (Jäger)**
    - **Pioneers**
    - **Railway & Telegraph Regiment**
    - **Artillery Staff**
- *(These breeches are not further detailed in the description.)*

-Summer Trousers

White or light drill summer trousers for **generals, officers, and officer deputies** are worn **only off-duty** and when enlisted men are in **linen drill trousers**.

Unbleached linen summer trousers for enlisted men are worn during **warm weather** for:

- **Regular foot drills**
- **Training exercises** (except when in marching order with field gear)
- **Barracks duties**
- **Off-duty wear**

Summer trousers **are not considered part of the formal military uniform** and thus are not further detailed in the following description.

-Field Blouse (Bluse)

In contrast to the **tunic (Waffenrock)**, the **field blouse** is the **standard field uniform** for **officers and enlisted men of infantry troops**, worn during:

Peacetime exercises - Marches - Drills - Off-duty

- *(For cavalry, see "Waffenrock.")*

Generals, adjutants, and aides-de-camp wear the blouse **only for office duty**, though this restriction is lifted in **southern regions**.

-Overcoat (Mantel)

The overcoat is worn in **cold or rainy weather**, for **parades, all service duties, and off-duty**.

It has **two rows of buttons**.

Officers' overcoats have:

- **No shoulder straps**
- **Piping** (for officers, military officials, cadet officer deputies, and military academy cadets)
- **Waist straps with two buttons**

Enlisted overcoats have:

- **Shoulder straps**
- **Waist straps with one button**

Officers may wear **fur-lined overcoats** in winter.

-Raincoat (Regenmantel)

Similar in **color and cut** to the overcoat but made of **waterproof material**, the raincoat is permitted for **generals and officers**.

-Cape (Radmantel / Pelerine)

Made of the same material as the overcoat (or loden cloth) and featuring a velvet collar like the overcoat, the **cape** reaches down to the knee. It may be worn by **all officers** (even over the overcoat) for **all duties—except parades—** as well as **off-duty**.

-Uniform Jackets (Waffenrock, Attila, Uhlanka) and Field Blouse (Bluse)

With few exceptions, these garments all have **stand-up collars**, on which **rank insignia** are displayed. **Overcoats**, however, have **fold-down collars**.

-Gaiters (Kamaschen)

Matching the color of the trousers (or summer trousers), gaiters may be worn for **all exercises—except parades**.

Officers wear them under the same conditions as enlisted men, as well as during **reconnaissance, training rides, and cycling**.

-Trouser band (Hosenbänder)

These **8 cm-wide bands**, matching the color of the trousers, are worn **especially in summer** as an alternative to gaiters.

-Gloves

Officers and NCOs are required to wear **white leather gloves**.

Officers may also wear **white kid gloves**.

Zugeteilter Dragoneroffizier.
Pionieroffizier in Bluse.

General. Generalstabsoffizier. Major vom Geniestab.
Offizier der reitenden Artillerie.

Dark brown gloves are permitted for officers:
- On the **riding grounds**
- During **off-duty rides**
- While **traveling by train**
- During **stays in the countryside**

-Spurs

All **mounted personnel** wear spurs—whether with **high boots (for riding breeches)** or **half-boots/shoes (for dress trousers)**.

Unmentioned Uniform Items

Uniform pieces not listed here—particularly those of the **Imperial and Royal Navy (k.u.k. Marine)**—are described in greater detail elsewhere.

-Uniform Materials

Generals, staff officers, and senior officers: Fine-quality cloth.

Officer deputies, cadets, and military academy students: Medium-quality cloth.

Enlisted men: Coarser cloth.

-One-Year Volunteers (Einjährig-Freiwillige)

They wear the **same uniforms as enlisted men** but may, at their own expense, have them made from **finer materials**—provided they adhere to regulations.

-Career NCOs (Extending Service Beyond Mandatory Duty)

They receive uniforms made of **semi-fine cloth**.

DESCRIPTION OF UNIFORMS

For Individual Military Personnel, Troops, Institutions, and Branches, etc., Including Armament Specifications.

General Officers (Generalität)
Generals in German Uniform

Gala Uniform

- **Hat:** Bicorne (two-pointed hat) with upturned brim (edged in gold braid), gold rosettes with the initials **F.J.I.**, and a hanging green **vulture-feather plume**.
- **Tunic (Waffenrock):** White, with **two rows of buttons**, **scarlet collar**, **cuffs**, and **piping**.
- **Trousers (Pantalon):** Scarlet, with **double gold stripes**.

Service Uniform

- **Hat:** As in Gala.
- **Field Cap (Feldkappe):** Black, with a visor, gold cord storm strap, and gold rosette with **F.J.I.**
- **Tunic (Waffenrock):** Pike-gray, with **two rows of buttons**, **scarlet collar**, **cuffs**, and **piping**.
- **Trousers (Pantalon):** Blue-gray, with **double scarlet stripes** and piping.
- **Riding Breeches (Stiefelhose):** Same as above, worn with **high boots and spurs**.
- **Field Blouse (Bluse):** Pike-gray, with **scarlet collar patches (Paroli)**.
- **Overcoat (Mantel):** Blue-gray, with a **velvet collar**, **scarlet patches**, **piping**, and lining.
- **Buttons:** Gilt, with embossed design.
- **Sidearm:** Infantry officer's saber with **gold hilt** and **gold sword knot**.

Generals in Hungarian Uniform

Gala Uniform

- **Busby (Kalpak):** Made of **marten fur**, with a **scarlet cloth bag**, **gold hanging cord with tassel**, and an upright **heron-feather plume**.
- **Attila (Jacket):** Scarlet, with **gold braiding**.
- **Fur Pelisse (Pelz):** White, with **gold braiding** and **marten fur trim** (worn slung over the shoulder).
- **Riding Breeches (Stiefelhose):** Scarlet, with **gold embroidery** and **double gold stripes**.
- **Boots (Czismen):** With **gold lacing**, **gold rosettes**, and **gilt spurs**.

Service Uniform

- **Shako (Czako):** Black, with a **gilt visor**, **gold cord decoration (Vitez Kötés)**, **gilt Imperial double eagle**, **gold rosette with F.J.I.**, and an upright **green vulture-feather plume**.
- **Field Cap (Feldkappe):** As in German uniform.
- **Attila (Jacket):** Pike-gray, with **gold braiding**, **scarlet collar**, and **cuffs**.
- **Winter Fur Pelisse (Pelz):** Pike-gray, with **gold braiding** and **sable fur trim**.
- **Trousers (Pantalon):** Blue-gray, with **double scarlet stripes** and piping.
- **Riding Breeches (Stiefelhose):** Same as above (close-fitting), worn with **plain boots and gilt spurs**.
- **Blouse (Bluse):** As in German uniform.
- **Overcoat (Mantel):** Dark brown, with a **velvet collar**, **scarlet patches**, **piping**, and lining.
- **Olives (Shoulder cords):** Gold braid.
- **Buttons:** As in German uniform.
- **Sidearm:** Same as German uniform.

Chief of the General Staff

- **Tunic (Waffenrock):** Dark green, with **two rows of buttons**, **black velvet collar and cuffs**, **scarlet piping**.
- **Gala Trousers (Pantalon):** Blue-gray, with **scarlet piping** and **double gold stripes**.
- **Blouse (Bluse):** Dark green, with **black velvet collar patches (Paroli)**, **scarlet-piped**.
- **All else:** As for generals in German uniform.

GENERAL AND AIDE-DE-CAMP
(General- und Flügel-Adjutanten)
General-Adjutants

- **Tunic (Waffenrock):** Dark green, with **two rows of buttons**, **scarlet collar**, **cuffs**, and **piping**.
- **Gala Trousers (Pantalon):** Dark green, with **scarlet piping** and **double gold stripes**.
- **Service Trousers:** Blue-gray, with **double scarlet stripes** and piping.
- **Blouse (Bluse):** Dark green, with **scarlet collar patches (Paroli)**.
- **All else:** As for generals in German uniform.

Note: When serving as **staff officers**, they generally follow the same regulations as **aides-de-camp**.

Aides-de-Camp (Flügel-Adjutanten)

- **Trousers (Pantalon):** Blue-gray, with **scarlet piping**; when mounted for parades, worn as **riding breeches**.
- **Buttons:**
  - For aides to **His Majesty**: Silver.
  - For those serving the **Imperial War Minister, field marshals**, and **army commanders**: Gilt.
- **All else:** As for **General-Adjutants**, but with **shorter collar patches on the blouse** and **gray liing in the overcoat**.

General Artillery Inspector

- **Tunic (Waffenrock):** Dark brown, with **two rows of buttons**, **scarlet collar**, **cuffs**, and **piping**.
- **Gala Trousers (Pantalon):** Light blue, with **scarlet piping** and **double gold stripes**.

- **Field Blouse (Bluse):** Dark brown, with **scarlet collar patches (Paroli)**.
- **All else:** As for generals in German uniform.

General Engineer Inspector

- **Tunic (Waffenrock):** Light blue, with **two rows of buttons**, **cherry-red velvet collar**, **cuffs**, and **piping**.
- **Gala Trousers (Pantalon):** Blue-gray, with **cherry-red velvet piping** and **double gold stripes**.
- **Service Trousers:** Blue-gray, with **cherry-red cloth stripes** and piping.
- **Field Blouse (Bluse):** Light blue, with **cherry-red velvet collar patches (Paroli)**.
- **All else:** As for generals in German uniform, but with **cherry-red distinctions on the overcoat**.

General Auditor

- **Hat:** Like generals in German uniform, but with a **hanging black cock-feather plume**.
- **Tunic (Waffenrock):**
  - **Gala:** White, with **two rows of buttons**, **madder-red collar**, **cuffs**, and **piping**.
  - **Service:** Black, with the same distinctions.
- **Trousers (Pantalon):**
  - **Gala:** Light blue, with **madder-red piping** and **double gold stripes**.
  - **Service:** Blue-gray, with **double madder-red stripes** and piping.
- **Field Blouse (Bluse):** Black, with **madder-red collar patches (Paroli)**.
- **Overcoat (Mantel):** Blue-gray, with a **velvet collar**, **madder-red patches**, and **piping**.
- **All else:** As for generals in German uniform.

General Staff Physician (Doctor)

- **Hat:** Like the General Auditor.
- **Tunic (Waffenrock):** Light blue, with **two rows of buttons**, **black velvet collar and cuffs**, **scarlet piping**.
- **Gala Trousers (Pantalon):** Blue-gray, with **scarlet piping** and **double gold stripes**.
- **Field Blouse (Bluse):** Light blue, with **black velvet collar patches (Paroli)**, **scarlet-piped**.
- **All else:** As for generals in German uniform (overcoat with **black piping**).

Military Officials with General Rank
General Intendant

- **Hat:** Like generals, but **no plume** and with a **different gold braid design**; brim edged with **short ostrich feathers**.
- **Tunic (Waffenrock):** Dark green, with **two rows of buttons**, **crimson velvet collar**, **cuffs**, and **piping**.
- **Trousers (Pantalon):**
  - **Gala:** Blue-gray, with **double gold stripes**.
  - **Service:** Blue-gray, with **double crimson cloth stripes** and piping.
- **Field Blouse (Bluse):** Dark green, with **crimson velvet collar patches (Paroli)**.
- **Overcoat (Mantel):** Blue-gray, with a **velvet collar**, **crimson velvet patches**, **piping**, and lining.
- **Sidearm:** Sword with **gilt hilt**, **gilt scabbard fittings**, **gold pommel**, and **gold sword knot**.
- **Field Cap & Buttons:** As for generals.

Artillery General Engineer

- **Hat:** Like the General Intendant.
- **Tunic, Blouse, Overcoat:** As for the **General Artillery Inspector**.
- **Trousers (Pantalon):**
  - **Gala:** Blue-gray, with **double gold stripes**.
  - **Service:** Blue-gray, with **double scarlet stripes** and piping.
- **All else:** As for the **General Intendant**.

General Construction Engineer

- **Hat:** Like the General Intendant.
- **Tunic, Blouse, Trousers, Overcoat:** As for the **General Engineer Inspector**.
- **All else:** As for the General Intendant.

Ministerial Councilors & Accounting Controllers

- **Hat:** Like the General Intendant.
- **Tunic (Waffenrock):** Dark green, with **two rows of buttons**, **alizarin-red collar**, **cuffs**, and **collar patches (Paroli)**.
- Trousers (Pantalon):
  - **Gala:** Blue-gray, with **double gold stripes**.
  - **Service:** Blue-gray, with **double alizarin-red stripes** and piping.
- **Field Blouse (Bluse):** Dark green, with **alizarin-red collar patches (Paroli)**.
- **Overcoat (Mantel):** Blue-gray, with a **velvet collar**, **alizarin-red patches**, **piping**, and lining.
- **All else:** As for the General Intendant.

IMPERIAL GUARDS (GARDEN)

1st Imperial Mounted Guard (k.u.k. 1. Arcieren-Leibgarde)

Court Service Uniform

- **Helmet:** Silver-plated, with **gilt Imperial double eagle** and **white buffalo-hair plume**.
- **Coat:** Poppy-red, **gold-braided**, with **gilt epaulettes (bullion-fringed)**, **black velvet collar and cuffs**.
- **Breeches:** Tight white buckskin.
- **Boots:** High riding boots with **strap-on spurs**.
- **Sidearm:** Saber with **gilt hilt**, **gold pommel**, and **gold sword knot**.

Standard Service Uniform

- **Field Cap:** Standard officer's cap.
- **Tunic (Waffenrock):** Black, with **two rows of buttons**, **scarlet collar**, **cuffs (gold-braided)**, and **piping**.
- **Trousers (Pantalon):** Blue-gray, with **scarlet piping**.
- **Field Blouse (Bluse):** Black, with **scarlet collar patches (Paroli)**.
- **Overcoat (Mantel):** White, with **scarlet collar**.
- **Buttons:** Gilt, smooth.
- **Sidearm:** Cavalry officer's saber with **gold pommel** and **gold sword knot**.

Imperial Foot Guards (k.k. Trabanten-Leibgarde)

Court Service Uniform

- **Spiked Helmet (Pickelhaube):** With **gilt Imperial double eagle** and **white buffalo-hair plume**.
- **Coat:** Similar to the Mounted Guard, but with an **additional black velvet breast panel** beneath the gold braiding.
- **Sidearm:** German sword with **gold knot (black for guardsmen)** and **halberd**.

Standard Service Uniform

- Generally as for the **1st Mounted Guard**.
- **For Sergeants (Feldwebel rank):** Gold elements replaced with **silk**, and **cap piping in red**.

Royal Hungarian Lifeguard (k. ung. Leibgarde)

Court Service Uniform

- **Busby (Kalpak):** Sable fur, with **green cloth bag** and **heron-feather plume**.
- **Attila (Jacket):** Bright red, with **silver braiding**.
- **Fur Pelisse:** Slung over the shoulder.
- **Breeches:** Tight, bright red, with **silver braiding**.
- **Cape (Radmantel):** White.
- **Boots (Czismen):** Yellow, with **silver lacing and spurs**.
- **Shoulder Cords (Oliven):** Silver.
- **Sidearm:** Hungarian (curved) saber with **silver fittings** and **silver knot**.

Standard Service Uniform

- **Attila & Blouse:** Dark green, with **silver braiding**.
- **Overcoat (Mantel):** Dark brown, with a **velvet collar** and **Attila-cloth distinctions**.
- **Buttons:** Smooth, silver-plated.
- **All else:** As for the **1st Mounted Guard**.

Royal Hungarian Bodyguard (Trabanten-Leibgarde)

(Established in 1904; not included in the color illustrations.)

- **Headgear:** *Kucsma* (Hungarian fur cap) with **poppy-red cloth bag** and **heron-feather plume**.
- **Attila (Jacket):** Dark green, with **poppy-red distinctions**, **gold braiding**, and **yellow shoulder cords (Oliven)**.
- **Trousers (Pantalon):** Blue-gray, with **poppy-red piping**.
- **Buttons:** Yellow, with **embossed design**.

Festungsartillerie.

Offizier der Landesschützen. Landwehrarzt Sanitätsoffizier.

Royal Hungarian Crown Guard (k. ung. Kronwache)

Court Service Uniform
- **Helmet:** Silver-plated, with **Royal Hungarian coat of arms** and **upright plume** (omitted for routine duties).
- **Neckcloth:** Black, with **silver fringe**.
- **Attila (Jacket):** Madder-red, with **silver braiding**.
- **Breeches:** Madder-red, with **silver braiding**.
- **Boots (Czismen):** Yellow.
- **Buttons (Oliven):** Smooth, silver-plated.
- **Sidearm:** Hungarian saber and **scythe-shaped halberd**.

Standard Service Uniform
- Generally as for the **Royal Hungarian Lifeguard**.

Imperial Royal Lifeguard Cavalry Squadron (k.u.k. Leibgarde-Reiter-Eskadron)

Court Service Uniform
- **Spiked Helmet (Pickelhaube):** With **gilt Imperial double eagle** and **black horsehair plume** (omitted for routine duties).
- **Tunic (Waffenrock):** Dark green, with **two rows of buttons, scarlet collar, cuffs,** and **piping**; **gilt shoulder cords** and **scale epaulettes**.
- **Breeches:** Tight white buckskin.
- **Boots:** High riding boots with **strap-on spurs**.
- **Sidearm:** Cavalry saber with **gold pommel** and **gold sword knot** (for NCOs: **black-and-yellow silk**).

Standard Service Uniform
- **Field Cap:** Standard officer's cap (for NCOs: **seam piping in red, silk cord and rosette**).
- **Tunic (Waffenrock):** Dark green, with **scarlet distinctions** and **gilt buttons** (two rows).
- **Trousers (Pantalon):** Blue-gray, with **scarlet piping**.
- **Field Blouse (Bluse):** Dark green, with **scarlet collar patches (Paroli)**.
- **Overcoat (Mantel):** White, with **scarlet collar and piping**.
- **Sidearm:** As for court service.
- **Buttons:** Yellow, smooth.

Royal Imperial Infantry Guard Company (k.k. Leibgarde-Infanterie-Kompagnie)

Court Service Uniform
- **Helmet (Pickelhaube)** and **Tunic (Waffenrock):** Same as the **Lifeguard Cavalry (Leibgarde-Reiter)**.
- **Trousers (Pantalon):** Dark green, with **scarlet piping**.
- **Overcoat (Mantel):** Blue-gray, with **scarlet collar patches (Paroli)** and **piping**.
- **NCO Belts:** As per infantry standards.
- **Armament:**
    - **Officers:** Infantry officer's saber with **gold pommel** and **gold sword knot**.
    - **NCOs:** Rifle with bayonet, **Gendarmerie saber (yellow grip)**.

Standard Service Uniform
- Generally as for the **Lifeguard Cavalry** (overcoat as in court dress).
- **Armament & Belts:** Same as court service uniform.
- **Buttons:** Yellow, smooth.

GENERAL STAFF

a) Imperial and Royal Army (k.u.k. Heer) and Imperial Reserve (k.k. Landwehr)

- **Tunic (Waffenrock):** Dark green, with **two rows of buttons**, **black velvet collar and cuffs**, **scarlet piping**.
- **Field Blouse (Bluse):** Dark green, with **black velvet collar patches (Paroli)** and **scarlet piping**.
- **Overcoat (Mantel):** Blue-gray, with **black velvet collar patches, scarlet piping**.
- **Buttons:** Gilt, smooth.
- **All else:** As for **Aides-de-Camp (Flügel-Adjutanten)**.

b) Royal Hungarian Reserve (königl. ung. Landwehr)

- **Shako (Czako):** Covered in **green cloth**, with **gold cord braid** and **upright green plume**.
- **Dolman (Waffenrock):** Dark green, with **black velvet collar and cuffs** trimmed in **gold braid** (Hungarian waist belt instead of sash).

Artillery Staff Officers (Est. 1907 – Not in Color Illustrations)

- **Trousers (Pantalon):** Blue-gray, with **scarlet piping**, worn as **riding breeches** for mounted parades.
- **All else:** As for **Field Artillery officers**.

Engineer Staff Officers

- **Hat:** Bicorne with **upturned brim**, edged in **black silk band** (gold for senior staff officers), **hanging cock-feather plume**, and **gold rosettes with F.J.I.**
- **Field Cap:** As for infantry officers.
- **Tunic (Waffenrock):** Light blue, with **two rows of buttons**, **cherry-red velvet collar, cuffs, and piping**.
- **Trousers (Pantalon):** Blue-gray, with **cherry-red velvet piping**, worn as **riding breeches** for mounted parades.
- **Field Blouse (Bluse):** Light blue, with **cherry-red velvet collar patches (Paroli)**.
- **Overcoat (Mantel):** Blue-gray, with **velvet collar, cherry-red velvet patches**, and **cloth piping**.
- **Buttons:** Yellow, smooth.
- **Armament:** Infantry officer's saber.

INFANTRY
Troops (102 Regiments)

Officers (See Regiment No. 1)

- **Shako (Czako):** Black, with **gilt visor**, **gilt Imperial double eagle**, and **gold rosette with F.J.I.**
- **Field Cap:** Standard officer's cap (black, with **visor, storm strap, gold cord**, and **gold rosette with F.J.I.**).
- **Tunic (Waffenrock):** Dark blue, with **one row of buttons**; **collar, cuffs, and piping** in **regimental distinction color** (Hungarian regiments: gold/silver lace on cuffs).
- **Trousers (Pantalon):** Light blue, worn as **riding breeches** for mounted parades/field duty.
- **Dress Trousers (Salonhose):** Blue-gray, with **scarlet piping**.
- **Field Blouse (Bluse):** Dark blue, with **regimental distinction-color collar patches (Paroli)**.
- **Overcoat (Mantel):** Blue-gray, with **velvet collar, regimental distinction patches**, and **piping**.
- **Buttons:** Smooth, gilt or silvered.
- **Armament:** Infantry officer's saber with **gold pommel** and **gold sword knot**.

Cadet Officer Deputies

- **Shako:** As for enlisted men.
- **All else:** Generally as for officers, but with:
  - **Cap cord & rosette, saber pommel & knot** in **black-yellow silk**.
  - **Tunic:** Shoulder straps in **distinction-color cloth**, **white cloth sleeve lace**.
  - **Overcoat:** Shoulder straps piped in **distinction color**, collar in **overcoat cloth**.

Enlisted Men

- **Shako (Czako):** Black, with **simple visor**, **brass Imperial double eagle**, and **rosette**.
- **Field Cap:** Light blue, with **visor** and **metal rosette with F.J.I.**
- **Tunic (Waffenrock):** Dark blue, with **one row of buttons**; **collar, cuffs, shoulder straps, and rolls in regimental distinction color** (Hungarian regiments: **white cloth lace on cuffs**).
- **Trousers:**
  - **German regiments:** Light blue.
  - **Hungarian regiments:** Tight light blue **cloth breeches**, decorated with **black-yellow wool cords**, worn with **infantry shoes (Czismen)**.
- **Field Blouse (Bluse):** Dark blue, with **matching shoulder straps** and **distinction-color collar patches (Paroli)**.
- **Overcoat (Mantel):** Blue-gray, with **shoulder straps** and **distinction-color patches**.
- **Buttons:** Smooth, yellow or white.
- **Belts:** Black, with **yellow buckle**.
- **Armament:**
  - **Riflemen:** Repeating rifle, **saber-bayonet**.
  - **Sergeants (Feldwebel):** Infantry officer's saber with **leather pommel**, **revolver**.
  - **Accountant NCOs & Musicians:** Infantry enlisted saber.
  - **Drummers, Pioneers, Medics:** Pioneer saber.
  - **Mounted Buglers:** Blue **riding breeches**, **high boots**, **cavalry belt**, saber as for sergeants.

Note: Mounted/long-serving NCOs, cadets, and buglers may wear **blue trousers** off-duty instead of breeches/Hungarian pants.

AUSTRO-HUNGARIAN INFANTRY REGIMENTS: DISTINCTION COLORS & BUTTON ASSIGNMENTS

Distinction Color	German Reg. (Yellow Buttons)	German Reg. (White Buttons)	Hungarian Reg. (Yellow Buttons)	Hungarian Reg. (White Buttons)	Distinction Color	German Reg. (Yellow Buttons)	German Reg. (White Buttons)	Hungarian Reg. (Yellow Buttons)	Hungarian Reg. (White Buttons)
White	94	92	–	–	OrangeYellow	99	41	16	101
Black	14	58	26	38	OrangeYellow	27	22	2	31
Scarlet	45	80	37	39	OrangeYellow	59	42	64	63
Amaranth	90	95	86	–	Light bleu	40	75	72	29
Krebs red	35	20	71	67	Light bleu	4	3	32	19
Krapp red	15	74	44	34	Pale Gray	100	98	–	–
Bordeaux	89	88	–	–	Ash-Gray	30	49	76	69
Blass red	57	36	65	66	Ash-Gray	11	24	51	33
Pale Pink	13	97	5	6	Apple-Green	21	87	70	25
Cherry red	73	77	43	23	Apple-Green	9	54	85	79
D.Crimson	84	81	96	82	Grass-Green	102	–	–	–
D. Crimson	1	18	52	53	Green	91	10	46	50
Dark Red	55	17	68	78	Steel-Green	8	28	61	62
Dark Red	93	7	12	83	Steel-Green	56	47	48	80

Regimental Distinctions

- **Collar/cuff colors & buttons** (silver/gold).
- **Hungarian regiments:** Additional **sleeve lace**; enlisted wear **corded breeches**.

Key Note:
- **Guards:** Elite distinctions (velvet, gold braid, plumes).
- **General Staff:** Dark green/black velvet, scarlet piping.
- **Infantry:** Dark blue with regimental colors (German/Hungarian variations).
- **NCOs/Cadets:** Simplified officer-style uniforms with silk/leather fittings. **Key Notes:**

-**Distinction Colors** (*Egalisierungsfarbe*): Determined **collar, cuffs, and piping** colors for each regiment.
-**Hungarian regiments** added **white sleeve lace** (not shown in table).
-**Buttons:** Yellow (gilt) or white (silvered) based on regiment type German units used **"deutsche Regimenter"**, Hungarian units **"ungar. Regimenter"**.
Special Cases: Black (No. 14, 58, 26, 38): Officers wore **velvet** collars/cuffs. **Dashes (–):** No regiments assigned to that category.

RIFLE TROOPS (JÄGER)
4 Tyrolean Imperial Rifle Regiments, 26 Field Rifle Battalions

Officers
- **Hat:** Black, with **gilt cord and acorns, cock-feather plume** on the left side, and a **gilt hunting horn emblem** (Tyrolean Imperial Rifles feature the **double eagle**, Field Rifles display **battalion numbers**).
- **Field Cap:** Same as infantry officers, with a **small horn emblem** at the front.
- **Tunic (Waffenrock):** Pike-gray, with **one row of buttons, grass-green collar, cuffs, and piping**.
- **Trousers (Pantalon):** Pike-gray, with **grass-green piping** and **double stripes**, worn as **riding breeches** for mounted parades/field duty.
- **Dress Trousers (Salonhose):** Blue-gray, with **grass-green piping**.
- **Field Blouse (Bluse):** Pike-gray, with **grass-green collar patches (Paroli)**.
- **Overcoat (Mantel):** Blue-gray, with a **velvet collar, grass-green patches**, and **piping**.
- **Buttons:** Gilt (smooth for Tyrolean Imperial Rifles, engraved with **battalion numbers** for Field Rifles).
- **Armament:** Same as infantry officers.

Cadet Officer Deputies
- Generally as for officers, but with:
  - **Hat cord:** Green.
  - **Cap cord & rosette, saber pommel & knot:** Black-yellow silk.
  - **Tunic:** Grass-green **shoulder straps**.
  - **Overcoat:** Piped shoulder straps, cloth collar.
  - **Trousers:** As for enlisted men.

Enlisted Men
- **Hat:** Black, with **green wool cord, cock-feather plume**, and **brass emblem** (same design as officers).
- **Field Cap:** Pike-gray, styled like infantry caps.
- **Tunic (Waffenrock):** Pike-gray, with **one row of buttons, grass-green collar, cuffs, shoulder straps, and rolls**.
- **Trousers (Pantalon):** Pike-gray, with **grass-green piping**.
- **Field Blouse (Bluse):** Pike-gray, with **grass-green collar patches (Paroli)**.
- **Overcoat (Mantel):** Blue-gray, with **grass-green patches**.
- **Buttons:** Yellow, otherwise as for officers.
- **Belts:** Black, as per infantry.
- **Armament:** Same as infantry enlisted men.

Regimental/Battalion Distinctions

- **Tyrolean Imperial Rifles: Double eagle** on hat emblem, **smooth buttons**.
- **Field Rifle Battalions: Battalion number** on hat emblem and buttons.
- **Buglers:** Deviations as per infantry; long-serving buglers may wear **trousers off-duty**

CAVALRY
Dragoons (15 Regiments)

Officers (See Regiment No. 1)

- **Helmet:** With **gilt Imperial double eagle**, **scale chinstrap**, and **comb**.
- **Field Cap:** As for infantry officers.
- **Tunic (Waffenrock):** Light blue, with **one row of buttons, collar, cuffs, and piping** in **regimental distinction color, gold shoulder cord**.
- **Fur Pelisse:** Lined collar, **two rows of buttons, gold hanging cord**.
- **Riding Breeches (Stiefelhose):** Crimson-red, with **high boots and spurs**.
- **Dress Trousers (Salonhose):** Blue-gray, with **crimson piping**.
- **Overcoat (Mantel):** Dark brown, with **velvet collar, regimental distinction patches**, and **piping**.
- **Buttons:** Smooth, gilt or silvered.
- **Armament:** Cavalry officer's saber with **gold pommel** and **gold sword knot**.

Cadet Officer Deputies

- **Helmet:** As for enlisted men.
- **All else:** As for officers, but with:
  - **Cords, rosette, saber fittings:** Black-yellow silk.
  - **Overcoat collar:** Cloth (not velvet).

Enlisted Men

- **Helmet:** With **yellow-metal Imperial double eagle, scale chinstrap**, and **combed edge**.
- **Field Cap:** Crimson-red, **no visor**, with **yellow metal rosette (F.J.I.)**.
- **Tunic (Waffenrock):** Light blue, with **one row of buttons, distinction-color collar and cuffs, yellow wool shoulder cord**.
- **Fur Pelisse:** Lined collar, **two rows of buttons, hanging cord**.
- **Riding Breeches (Stiefelhose):** Crimson-red, with **high boots and spurs**.
- **Overcoat (Mantel):** Dark brown, with **distinction-color patches**.
- **Buttons:** Smooth, yellow or white.
- **Armament:**
  - **Cavalry saber, repeating carbine**.
  - **NCOs: Revolver** or **repeating pistol** instead of carbine.
- **Long-serving NCOs:** May wear **blue-gray trousers with crimson piping** off-duty.

Regimental Distinctions

- **Collar/cuff colors & buttons** (silver/gold)

Key Features:

- **Rifle Troops:** Grass-green distinctions, hunting horn emblems.
- **Dragoons:** Light blue tunics, crimson breeches, fur pelisses.
- **Buttons & Emblems:** Denote Tyrolean/Field Rifle or specific regiments.
- **NCOs/Cadets:** Simplified officer-style uniforms with silk/wool fittings.

CAVALRY REGIMENTAL DISTINCTIONS: COLLAR COLORS & BUTTONS

Distinction Color	Yellow Buttons (Regiment Nr.)	White Buttons (Regiment Nr.)	Distinction Color	Yellow Buttons (Regiment Nr.)	White Buttons (Regiment Nr.)
Black (Velvet for Officers)	6	2	Sulfur-Yellow	7	–
Scarlet-Red	8	11	Imperial-Yellow	2	5
Madder-Red	11	13	Grass-Green	9	4

Key Notes:

-**Distinction Colors** (*Egalisierung*): Determined **collar and cuff colors** for each regiment. **Black (No. 6, 2):** Officers wore **velvet** collars.

-**Buttons: Yellow (gilt)** or **White (silvered)** based on regiment. Example: **Scarlet-Red:** Regiment 8 (yellow buttons), Regiment 11 (white buttons). **Grass-Green:** Regiment 9 (yellow buttons), Regiment 4 (white buttons).

-**Special Cases: Sulfur-Yellow (No. 7):** Only listed with **yellow buttons**. **Dashes (–):** No regiments assigned to that combination.

Hussars (16 Regiments)

Officers (See Regiment No. 1)

- **Shako (Czako):** Varies in color, with an **upright black horsehair plume, gold rosette (F.J.I.), Imperial double eagle with regimental number**, and **gold cord decoration (Vitez-Kötés)**.
- **Field Cap:** Same as infantry officers.
- **Winter Attila:** Light blue or dark blue, with **black fur trim, fold-down collar**, and **gold braiding** (fur-lined).
- **Summer Attila:** Same as winter, but **without fur trim** (no distinction colors).
- **Riding Breeches (Stiefelhose):** Tight crimson-red, with **gold embroidery**, worn with **Hungarian boots (Czismen) and spurs**.
- **Dress Trousers (Salonhose):** Blue-gray, with **crimson piping**.
- **Overcoat (Mantel):** Dark brown, with **velvet collar, Attila-cloth patches**, and **piping**.
- **Buttons (Oliven):** Smooth, gilt or silvered.
- **Armament:** Same as dragoon officers.

Cadet Officer Deputies

- **Shako & Buttons:** As for enlisted men.
- **All else:** As for officers, but with:
  - **Cap cord & rosette, braiding, saber fittings:** Black-yellow silk.
  - **Overcoat collar:** Cloth (not velvet).

Enlisted Men

- **Shako (Czako):** Like officers, but with **simplified brass rosette and eagle, yellow wool cord decoration** (trumpeters: **red horsehair plume**).
- **Field Cap:** Same as dragoon enlisted.
- **Winter Attila:** Light blue or dark blue, with **black fur trim, fold-down collar**, and **yellow wool braiding**.
- **Summer Attila:** Not issued to enlisted men.
- **Riding Breeches (Stiefelhose):** Tight crimson-red, with **yellow wool braiding**, worn with **Czismen and spurs**.
- **Overcoat (Mantel):** Dark brown, with **Attila-cloth patches**.
- **Buttons (Oliven):** Smooth, yellow or white.
- **Armament:** Same as dragoon enlisted.
- **Long-Serving NCOs:** Permitted to wear **blue-gray trousers with crimson piping** off-duty (as for dragoons).

Regimental Distinctions

- Shako color, Attila/Blouse/Overcoat distinction colors, buttons, and numbers on shako eagle.

HUSSAR REGIMENTAL DISTINCTIONS TABLE

Shako Cover Color	Dark Blue Attila Blouse & Overcoat Distinction Colors		Light Blue Attila Blouse & Overcoat Distinction Colors	
	Olive buttons			
Crimson-Red	8 (Yellow)	5 (White)	14 (Yellow)	4 (White)
White	3 (Yellow)	9 (White)	2 (Yellow)	12 (White)
Dark Blue	1 (Yellow)	13 (White)	–	–
Light Blue	–	–	10 (White)	7 (White)
Ash-Gray	15 (Yellow)	11 (White)	6 (Yellow)	16 (White)

Key Notes:
- **Shako Cover Colors:** Determined the **base color of the shako** (e.g., crimson-red, white, dark blue).
- **Attila Types: Dark Blue Attila:** Worn by regiments with yellow/white buttons (e.g., No. 1, 8, 15). **Light Blue Attila:** Worn by regiments with white buttons (e.g., No. 5, 9, 11).
- **Blouse & Overcoat Distinctions:** Listed by **regiment number** and **button color** (yellow/white). Example: **Crimson shako (No. 14):** Yellow distinctions. **White shako (No. 2):** Yellow distinctions.
- **Buttons (Oliven): Yellow (gilt)** or **White (silvered). Ash-Gray shako regiments:** Included button colors (No. 12: white).
- **Dashes (–):** No regiments assigned to that combination.

Uhlans (Lancers) (11 Regiments)

Officers

- **Czapka (Lancer Cap):** Varies in color, featuring a **gilt Imperial double eagle (with regimental number), scale chinstrap, gold braiding,** and a **hanging horsehair plume secured by gilt chain links.** Includes a **gold rosette with "F.J.I."**.
- **Field Cap:** Same as infantry officers.
- **Uhlanka (Lancer Tunic):** Light blue, with **one row of buttons, piped pocket flaps, crimson-red collar, cuffs, and piping, gold shoulder cord,** and **gold bullion fringe between rear waist buttons**.
- **Fur Uhlanka:** Fur-trimmed fold-down collar, **two rows of buttons,** and **gold hanging cord**.
- **Riding Breeches (Stiefelhose):** Crimson-red, worn with **high boots and spurs**.
- **Dress Trousers (Salonhose):** Blue-gray, with **crimson piping**.
- **Overcoat (Mantel):** Dark brown, with **velvet collar, crimson patches,** and **piping**.
- **Buttons (Kompasseln):** Smooth, gilt or silvered.
- **Armament:** Same as dragoon officers.

Cadet Officer Deputies

- **Czapka & Buttons:** As for enlisted men.
- **All else:** As for officers, but with:
    - **Cords, rosettes, fringe, sword fittings:** Black-yellow silk.
    - **Overcoat collar:** Cloth (not velvet).

Enlisted Men

- **Czapka:** Similar to officers, but with **brass eagle, chinstrap, rosette, and chain links**. NCOs have **black-yellow wool trim**; trumpeters wear a **red horsehair plume**.
- **Field Cap:** Same as dragoon enlisted.
- **Uhlanka:** Light blue, with **one row of buttons, piped pocket flaps, crimson collar, cuffs, and piping,** and **black-yellow wool shoulder cord**.

- **Fur Uhlanka:** Fur-trimmed fold-down collar and **two rows of buttons**.
- **Riding Breeches (Stiefelhose):** Crimson-red, with **high boots and spurs**.
- **Overcoat (Mantel):** Dark brown, with **crimson patches**.
- **Buttons (Kompasseln):** Smooth, yellow or white.
- **Armament:** Same as dragoon enlisted.
- **Long-Serving NCOs:** Permitted to wear **blue-gray trousers with crimson piping** off-duty (as for dragoons).

Regimental Distinctions

- **Buttons (Kompasseln)** and **Czapka colors**, plus **numbers on the czapka eagle**.

Key Features:

-**Czapka:** Distinctive lancer cap with regimental colors/plumes.

-**Uhlanka:** Light blue with crimson accents; fur-lined for winter.

-**Breeches:** Crimson with high boots (officers: gold fringe; enlisted: wool cords).

-**Buttons & Braiding:** Gilt/silver for officers, brass/yellow wool for enlisted.

UHLAN (LANCER) REGIMENTAL DISTINCTIONS TABLE

Buttons (Kompasseln)	Czapka Cover Colors						
	Imperial Yellow	Dark Green	Crimson Red	White	Light Blue	Cherry Red	Dark bleu
Yellow	1	2	3	4	5	–	12
White	6	7	8	–	–	11	13

Note: Regiments No. 9 and 10 were disbanded or converted into Dragoon and Hussar regiments, respectively.

Key Details:

-**Button Colors (Kompasseln):** Yellow (gilt) or White (silvered).

-**Shako Cover Colors:**-Each regiment had a distinct shako cover color (e.g., **Imperial Yellow, Dark Blue, Crimson Red**).

-**Regimental Assignments:** Example: **Imperial Yellow shako:** Yellow buttons: **Regiment 1** White buttons: **Regiment 6 Dark Blue shako:** Yellow buttons: **Regiment 2** White buttons: **Regiment 7**

-**Disbanded Units:** Regiments **9** and **10** were dissolved or reassigned to other cavalry branches.

ARTILLERY
Field Artillery

(14 field howitzer regiments, 42 field cannon regiments, 8 mounted battalion divisions, 9 heavy howitzer divisions, and 6 mountain artillery regiments.)

Officers

- **Czako (shako):** Black, with a gilded imperial double eagle, gold rosette, and a hanging horsehair plume secured by a gilded chain.
- **Field cap:** Same as infantry officers.
- **Tunic:** Dark brown, with a single row of buttons; collar, cuffs, and piping in scarlet; gold shoulder cords and hanging cord.
- **Breeches:** Light blue, worn with high boots and spurs.
- **Dress trousers:** Blue-gray with scarlet piping.
- **Overcoat:** Blue-gray with velvet collar, scarlet paroli (trim) and piping.
- **Buttons:** Gilded, with a cannon emblem (crossed cannon barrels with a rocket).
- **Armament:** Same as dragoon officers.

Cadet Officer Deputies

- **Czako**: Same as enlisted men.
- **All else**: Same as officers, but cords and tassels, sword knot, and porte-épée in black-and-yellow silk; overcoat collar in cloth.

Enlisted Men

- **Czako**: Generally like officers, but with brass eagle, rosette, and chain (trumpeters have a red horse hair plume).
- **Field cap**: Light blue, with a visor and rosette (mounted battery divisions without a visor).
- **Tunic**: Dark brown, single row of buttons; collar, cuffs, shoulder straps, and rolls in scarlet; NCOs also have a brown hanging cord.
- **Breeches**: Light blue, with high boots and spurs.
- **Trousers for dismounted troops**: Light blue with scarlet piping.
- **Overcoat**: Blue-gray with scarlet paroli.
- **Buttons**: Yellow metal, with cannon emblem.
- **Armament**:
    - **NCOs**: Cavalry enlisted saber and revolver or repeating pistol.
    - **Gunners**: Pioneer saber, some with repeating carbines.
    - **Mounted batteries**: Light cavalry sabers, revolvers (or repeating pistols); drivers carry pioneer sabers.
    - Long-serving NCOs may wear trousers instead of breeches.

Fortress Artillery
(6 regiments and 3 battalions.)

Officers

- **Trousers**: Light blue with scarlet piping (adjusted as breeches when mounted).
- **Dress trousers**: Blue-gray with scarlet piping.
- **Otherwise**: Same as field artillery officers, but without a hanging cord on the tunic. Buttons gilded with cannon emblem.

Cadet Officer Deputies

- **Czako and trousers**: Like enlisted men.
- **All else**: Like officers, but cords, etc., as per field artillery cadet officer deputies.

Enlisted Men

- **Trousers**: Light blue with scarlet piping.
- **Otherwise**: Same as field artillery enlisted, but without breeches and high boots.
- **Buttons**: Yellow, with cannon emblem.
- **Armament**:
    - **Fireworkers**: Cavalry enlisted saber.
    - **Others**: Repeating carbine with bayonet, some with pioneer sabers.

Technical Artillery

Officers

- **All items**: Like fortress artillery officers, but without breeches and high boots. The czako eagle bears a "T," and the tunic has no hanging cord.
- **Buttons**: Gilded, with cannon emblem.

Enlisted Men

- **Czako**: Like infantry enlisted, with a "T" on the eagle.
- **Field cap**: Light blue, with visor and rosette (F.J.I.).
- **Trousers**: Light blue with scarlet piping.

- **Tunic and overcoat**: Like fortress artillery.
- **Buttons**: Yellow, with cannon emblem.
- **Armament**:
  - **Fireworkers**: Cavalry enlisted saber.
  - **Others**: Pioneer saber with fixed knot.

PIONEER TROOPS
(15 battalions.)

Officers
- **Czako and field cap**: Like infantry officers.
- **Tunic**: Pike-gray, single row of buttons; collar, cuffs, and piping in steel-green cloth.
- **Trousers**: Pike-gray with steel-green piping and stripes (adjusted as breeches when mounted).
- **Dress trousers**: Blue-gray with steel-green piping.
- **Blouse**: Pike-gray with steel-green paroli.
- **Overcoat**: Blue-gray with velvet collar, steel-green paroli and piping.
- **Buttons**: Silvered and smooth.
- **Armament**: Like infantry officers.

Cadet Officer Deputies
- **Czako and trousers**: Like enlisted men.
- **Otherwise**: Like officers, but cap cords, rosette, sword knot, and porte-épée in black-and-yellow silk; tunic shoulder straps in steel-green cloth; overcoat collar in cloth.

Enlisted Men
- **Czako**: Like infantry enlisted.
- **Field cap**: Pike-gray, with visor and rosette (F.J.I.).
- **Tunic**: Pike-gray, single row of buttons; collar, cuffs, shoulder straps, and rolls in steel-green.
- **Trousers**: Pike-gray with steel-green piping.
- **Blouse**: Pike-gray with steel-green paroli.
- **Overcoat**: Blue-gray with steel-green paroli.
- **Buttons**: White metal, smooth.
- **Equipment**: Black leather.
- **Armament**: Repeating carbine with bayonet, some with pioneer sabers; otherwise like infantry.

Railway and Telegraph Regiment
(1 regiment.)

Officers
- **All items**: Like pioneer officers, with special insignia:
  - **Winged wheels**: Gold-embroidered, on both collar ends of the tunic and blouse (behind rank stars); wings face backward, with jagged lightning bolts radiating from the axle.

Cadet Officer Deputies
- **All items**: Like pioneer officer deputies, with enlisted insignia.

Enlisted Men
- **All items**: Like pioneer enlisted, with silver winged wheels (as per officers) on collar ends of tunic and blouse (behind rank stars for NCOs).

Medical Troops
(26 detachments.)

Officers
- **Czako and field cap**: Like infantry officers.

- **Tunic**: Dark green, single row of buttons; collar, cuffs, and piping in crimson.
- **Trousers**: Blue-gray with crimson piping (adjusted as breeches when mounted).
- **Blouse**: Dark green with crimson paroli.
- **Overcoat**: Blue-gray with velvet collar, crimson paroli and piping.
- **Buttons**: Gilded and smooth.
- **Armament**: Like infantry officers.

Cadet Officer Deputies
- **Czako**: Like enlisted men.
- **Otherwise**: Like officers, but cords, rosette, sword knot, and porte-épée in black-and-yellow silk; tunic shoulder straps in crimson; overcoat collar in cloth.

Enlisted Men
- **Czako**: Like infantry enlisted.
- **Field cap**: Blue-gray, with visor and rosette (F.J.I.).
- **Tunic**: Dark green, single row of buttons; collar, cuffs, and shoulder straps in crimson.
- **Trousers**: Blue-gray.
- **Blouse**: Dark green with crimson paroli.
- **Overcoat**: Blue-gray with crimson paroli.
- **Buttons**: Yellow, smooth.
- **Equipment**: Black leather.
- **Armament**: Pioneer saber.

Train Troops
(3 regiments.)

Officers
- **Czako and field cap**: Like artillery officers.
- **Tunic**: Dark brown, single row of buttons; collar, cuffs, and piping in light blue; gold shoulder cord and hanging cord.
- **Breeches**: Crimson, with high boots and spurs.
- **Dress trousers**: Blue-gray with crimson piping.
- **Overcoat**: Dark brown with velvet collar, light blue paroli and piping.
- **Buttons**: Silvered and smooth.
- **Armament**: Like dragoon officers.

Cadet Officer Deputies
- **Czako**: Like enlisted men.
- **Otherwise**: Like officers, but cords, rosette, sword knot, and porte-épée in black-and-yellow silk; overcoat collar in cloth.

Enlisted Men (Field Squadrons and Train Depots)
- **Czako**: Like artillery enlisted.
- **Field cap**: Like dragoon enlisted.
- **Tunic**: Dark brown, single row of buttons; collar and cuffs in light blue; NCOs have black-and-yellow wool shoulder cords.
- **Breeches**: Crimson, with high boots and spurs.
- **Overcoat**: Dark brown with light blue paroli.
- **Buttons**: White metal, smooth.
- **Armament**:
  - **NCOs**: Cavalry enlisted saber.
  - **Enlisted**: Pioneer saber, repeating carbine.
  - Long-serving NCOs may wear blue-gray trousers (like officers' dress trousers).

Enlisted Men (Mountain Train Squadrons)
- **Field cap**: Like infantry.
- **Breeches**: Light blue for NCOs, with high boots and spurs.
- **Trousers**: Light blue for soldiers.
- **Overcoat**: Blue-gray with light blue paroli.
- **Armament**:
  - **Sergeants**: Cavalry enlisted saber.
  - **Others**: Pioneer saber.
- **Otherwise**: Like field squadron enlisted.

Master Craftsmen of Train Depots
- **Cap (instead of czako)**: Light blue, officer-style, with rosette and rank braid in black-and-yellow wool.
- **Armament**: Cavalry enlisted saber.
- **Otherwise**: Like field squadron NCOs.

Uniform Administration Branch

Officers
- **Czako**: Like infantry officers.
- **Tunic**: Dark green, single row of buttons; collar, cuffs, and piping in russet.
- **Trousers**: Blue-gray with russet piping.
- **Blouse**: Dark green with russet paroli.
- **Overcoat**: Blue-gray with velvet collar, russet paroli and piping.
- **Buttons**: Gilded and smooth.
- **Armament**: Like infantry officers.

Enlisted Men
- **Cap (instead of czako)**: Blue-gray, officer-style, with rosette and rank braid (for NCOs) in black-and-yellow wool.
- **Field cap**: Blue-gray, otherwise like infantry.
- **Tunic**: Dark green, single row of buttons; russet collar, cuffs, and shoulder straps.
- **Trousers**: Blue-gray.
- **Blouse**: Dark green with russet paroli.
- **Buttons**: Yellow, smooth.
- **Armament**: Infantry enlisted saber, carried on a fixed knot.

Commissariat Branch

Enlisted Men
- **Czako**: Like infantry enlisted.
- **Field cap**: Pike-gray, with visor and rosette (F.J.I.).
- **Tunic**: Pike-gray, single row of buttons; light blue collar, cuffs, and shoulder straps.
- **Trousers**: Pike-gray.
- **Blouse**: Pike-gray with light blue paroli.
- **Overcoat**: Blue-gray with light blue paroli.
- **Equipment**: Black leather.
- **Armament**: Repeating carbine with bayonet; some carry infantry enlisted sabers.

Military-Geographical Institute

Enlisted Men
- **Czako**: Like infantry enlisted.
- **Field cap**: Blue-gray, like infantry.

- **Tunic**: Dark green, single row of buttons; scarlet collar, shoulder straps, and cuffs.
- **Trousers**: Blue-gray with scarlet piping.
- **Blouse**: Dark green with scarlet paroli.
- **Overcoat**: Blue-gray with scarlet paroli.
- **Buttons**: Yellow, smooth.
- **Equipment**: Black leather.
- **Armament**:
  - **Enlisted**: Infantry enlisted saber.
  - **NCOs**: Officer saber (like officer deputies), but with knot in Isfahan wool.

Officers of the Army Staff
- **Hat**: With cock feather plume, like General Staff officers.
- **Tunic**: Black, double row of buttons; scarlet collar, cuffs, and piping.
- **Trousers**: Blue-gray with scarlet piping (adjusted as breeches when mounted).
- **Blouse**: Black with scarlet paroli.
- **Otherwise**: Like infantry officers, with scarlet trim.
- **Buttons**: Yellow, smooth.

Commissary Officers Corps
(Est. 1906 – not included in color plates.)
- **Hat**: With cock feather plume, like General Staff officers.
- **Field cap**: Like infantry officers.
- **Tunic**: Dark brown, double row of buttons; light blue collar, cuffs, and piping.
- **Trousers**: Blue-gray with light blue piping (adjusted as breeches when mounted).
- **Blouse**: Dark brown with light blue paroli.
- **Overcoat**: Blue-gray with velvet collar, light blue paroli and piping.
- **Buttons**: White, smooth.
- **Armament**: Like infantry officers.

Commissary Officer Deputies
- Generally like commissary officers, but hat and cap rosette, cords, sword knot, and porte-épée in black-and-yellow silk; overcoat collar in cloth; tunic, blouse, and overcoat with shoulder straps.

Invalid and Veterans' Corps

Officers
- **Hat**: With cock feather plume, like General Staff officers.
- **Field cap**: Like infantry officers.
- **Tunic**: Pike-gray, double row of buttons; crimson collar, cuffs, and piping.
- **Trousers**: Light blue.
- **Dress trousers**: Blue-gray with crimson piping.
- **Blouse**: Pike-gray with crimson paroli.
- **Overcoat**: Blue-gray with velvet collar, crimson paroli and piping.
- **Buttons**: White, smooth.
- **Armament**: Like infantry officers.

Enlisted Men
- **Cap**: Pike-gray, officer-style, with a 3 cm-wide crimson stripe, rosette, and cord in black-and-yellow wool.
- **Tunic**: Pike-gray, double row of buttons; crimson collar, cuffs, and shoulder straps.
- **Trousers**: Light blue.

- **Overcoat**: Blue-gray with crimson paroli.
- **Buttons**: White, smooth.
- **Armament**: Infantry enlisted saber, worn on a black cross-belt.

Staff and Senior Officers in Retirement or Reserve

These wear the uniform of their last assigned unit but without a field sash (ammo pouch), so shoulder cords (for cavalry, etc.) are omitted.

Generals: Same as active generals, including the field sash.

Military Bandmasters

- **Hat**: With cock feather plume, like General Staff officers; hat rosette and cord in silver.
- **Field cap**: Like infantry officers, but rosette and cord in silver with red.
- **Tunic**: Black, single row of buttons; collar, cuffs, and piping in regimental facing color (silver braid for Hungarian regiments).
- **Trousers**: Blue-gray with piping in regimental facing color.
- **Blouse**: Black with paroli in regimental facing color.
- **Overcoat**: Blue-gray with velvet collar, paroli and piping in regimental facing color.
- **Buttons**: Gilded or silvered, smooth.
- **Armament**: Infantry officer saber with silver knot and silver porte-épée (red threading).

(Illustration based on Infantry Regiment No. 84.)

Military Educational Institutions
A. Cadets
(All items of medium quality)

Cadet Schools
Infantry Cadet Schools

- Uniform as per **Infantry Regiment No. 1**.
- **Field cap**: Like cadet officer deputies.
- **Tunic & overcoat**: Same as cadet officer deputies, with piping.

Detachment for Train Troops *(in 2 cadet schools)*

- Generally like **Train Troops enlisted men**, plus:
  - **Trousers**: Blue-gray with crimson piping.
  - **Field cap**: Like cadet officer deputies.
  - **Tunic & overcoat**: Same as cadet officer deputies, with piping.

Cavalry Cadet School

- Uniform as per **Hussar Regiment No. 1**, but:
  - **Summer Attila**: With fine yellow wool braiding.
  - **Breeches & dress trousers**: Like hussar officers.
  - **Field cap**: Like cadet officer deputies.

Artillery Cadet School

- Uniform like **Fortress Artillery enlisted men**, including **cannon-emblazoned buttons**.
- **Field cap**: Like cadet officer deputies.
- **Tunic & overcoat**: Same as cadet officer deputies, with piping.

Pioneer Cadet School

- Uniform like **Pioneer Troops enlisted men**.
- **Cap**: Like cadet officer deputies.
- **Tunic & overcoat**: Same as cadet officer deputies, with piping.
- **Trousers**: With dark green single-stripe lampasse.

Attached Enlisted Personnel in All Cadet Schools
- Generally like cadets, but **without blue-gray trousers** (for cavalry and train personnel).

Officers' Orphan Institute
- **Cap**: Black, officer-style, with black-yellow silk cord/rosette, yellow buttons.
- **Blouse**: Dark gray, two breast pockets, scarlet paroli.
- **Trousers**: Dark gray.
- **Overcoat**: Blue-gray, scarlet paroli, yellow buttons.
- **Summer uniform**: Gray twill.
- **Armament**: None.

Military Lower Realschulen
- **Cap**: Dark gray, otherwise like the Orphan Institute.
- **Tunic**: Dark gray, scarlet collar, shoulder straps, cuffs, and piping.
- **Trousers**: Light blue.
- **Blouse**: Dark blue, scarlet paroli.
- **Overcoat**: Blue-gray, scarlet paroli/piping.
- **Buttons**: Yellow, smooth.
- **Armament**: None.

Military Upper Realschulen
- **Shako**: Like infantry enlisted men.
- **Tunic**: As per Lower Realschulen.
- **Equipment**: Black leather.
- **Armament**: Like infantry enlisted men.
- **Otherwise**: Same as Lower Realschulen.

Military Academies
- Same as Upper Realschulen, except:
  - **Technical Academy cadets**: Carry **pioneer sabers**.
  - **Senior year cadets**: Gold stripes on sleeves; off-duty, they wear **officer sabers** like officer deputies.

Cadet Distinctions in All Institutions
- **Collar distinctions**:
  - **Good progress**: 1 stripe (gold in academies, silver in Pioneer Cadet School, yellow silk elsewhere).
  - **Very good**: 2 stripes.
  - **Excellent**: 2 stripes + 2 buttons (*Cadet NCO*).
- **Shako distinctions**:
  - **Upper Realschule & Cadet Schools**: Corporal braid for single distinction; Sergeant braid for double distinction or Cadet NCOs.
  - **Academies**: All cadets wear Sergeant braid.

B. Teaching & Supervisory Staff

Instructors, Inspectors, and Drill Sergeants (*All educational institutions*)
- **Shako**: Like infantry enlisted men.
- **Cap**: Like cadets.
- **Tunic**: Dark gray, single-button row, scarlet collar/cuffs.
- **Trousers**: Light blue.
- **Blouse**: Dark blue, scarlet paroli.

- **Overcoat**: Blue-gray, scarlet paroli.
- **Buttons**: Yellow, smooth.
- **Armament**: Infantry officer saber, black-yellow wool knot/porte-épée.

Riding Instructor Assistants

a) Riding Instructor Institute, Military Academy, War School *(NCOs)*
- **Field cap**: Like cadets.
- **Tunic**: Light blue, single-button row, crimson collar/cuffs.
- **Buttons**: Yellow, smooth.
- **Otherwise**: Like dragoon enlisted men.
- **Optional**: Blue-gray trousers with crimson piping.

b) Technical Military Academy
- **Field cap**: Like cadets.
- **Tunic**: Dark brown, single-button row, scarlet collar/cuffs.
- **Blouse**: Dark blue, scarlet paroli.
- **Buttons**: Yellow, cannon emblem.
- **Otherwise**: Like field artillery enlisted men.
- **Optional**: Light blue trousers with scarlet piping.

C. Enlisted Personnel

Musicians
- **Tunic**: Dark gray, single-button row, scarlet collar/cuffs/shoulder straps.
- **Buttons**: Yellow, smooth.
- **Otherwise**: Like infantry enlisted men with scarlet trim.

Orderlies
- **Cap**: Dark gray, officer-style, 3 cm scarlet stripe, black-yellow wool rosette.
- **Tunic**: Dark gray, single-button row, scarlet collar/shoulder straps/cuffs.
- **Trousers**: Dark gray.
- **Blouse**: Dark blue, scarlet paroli.
- **Buttons**: Yellow, smooth.
- **Armament**: Infantry enlisted saber.

Military Veterinary Institute

Officers
- Wear the uniform of the branch they are assigned to.

Enlisted Personnel
- **Cap** (instead of shako): Light blue, officer-style, with black-and-yellow wool rosette and rank braid (for NCOs).
- **Field cap**: Like infantry enlisted men.
- **Tunic**: Dark brown, single row of buttons, light blue collar and cuffs; NCOs wear a black-and-yellow wool shoulder cord.
- **Breeches**: Light blue, with high boots and spurs.
- **Blouse**: Dark blue, light blue paroli.
- **Overcoat**: Dark brown, light blue paroli.
- **Buttons**: Yellow, smooth.
- **Armament**: Cavalry enlisted saber.

Military Chaplains (Catholic)

Parade Dress
- **Military hat**: Like General Staff officers, but without plume and with gold tassels instead of rosettes.
- **Cassock** with clerical collar and black silk sash with gold fringe.
- **Abbé overcoat**: Black silk.

Field Dress
- **Field cap**: Like infantry officers.
- **Clerical coat and collar**.
- **Overcoat**: Blue-gray with black velvet paroli and black cloth piping; yellow smooth buttons.
- **Trousers**: Black.

Note: Chaplains of other faiths (Protestant ministers, rabbis, etc.) wear military attire similar to Catholic chaplains, adjusted per their religious regulations.

Auditors
- **Hat**: With cock feather plume, like General Staff officers.
- **Field cap**: Like infantry officers.
- **Tunic**: Black, double row of buttons, crimson collar, cuffs, and piping.
- **Trousers**: Blue-gray with crimson piping.
- **Bluse**: Black with crimson paroli.
- **Overcoat**: Blue-gray with velvet collar, crimson paroli and piping.
- **Buttons**: Yellow, smooth.
- **Armament**: Like infantry officers.

Military Physicians
- **Hat**: With cock feather plume, like General Staff officers.
- **Field cap**: Like infantry officers.
- **Tunic**: Light blue, double row of buttons, black velvet collar and cuffs with scarlet piping.
- **Trousers**: Blue-gray with scarlet piping.
- **Bluse**: Light blue with black velvet paroli.
- **Overcoat**: Blue-gray with black velvet paroli and black cloth piping.
- **Buttons**: Yellow, smooth.
- **Armament**: Like infantry officers.

Assistant Physician Deputies
- **Hat**: Like physicians, but with silk rosettes.
- **Field cap**: Like infantry officer deputies.
- **Tunic**: Light blue, as per physicians.
- **Armament**: Like infantry cadet officer deputies.
- **Otherwise**: Same as military physicians.

Troop Paymasters
- **Hat**: With cock feather plume, like General Staff officers.
- **Field cap**: Like infantry officers.
- **Tunic**: Dark green, double row of buttons, light blue collar, cuffs, and piping.
- **Trousers**: Blue-gray with light blue piping.
- **Bluse**: Dark green with light blue paroli.
- **Overcoat**: Blue-gray with velvet collar, light blue paroli and piping.

- **Buttons**: White, smooth.
- **Armament**: Like infantry officers.

Paymaster Deputies

- Same as paymasters, but:
  - Hat and cap rosettes, cords, sword knot, and porte-épée in black-and-yellow silk.
  - Overcoat collar in cloth.
  - Shoulder straps on tunic, blouse, and overcoat.

Military Officials

(Note: Whether they carry a porte-épée and wear stars or rosettes is specified below.)

Intendance Officials

- **Hat**: Like General Staff officers, but without plume.
- **Field cap**: Like infantry officers.
- **Tunic**: Dark green, double row of buttons, crimson velvet collar, cuffs, and piping.
- **Trousers**: Blue-gray with crimson velvet piping.
- **Bluse**: Dark green with crimson velvet paroli.
- **Overcoat**: Blue-gray with velvet collar, crimson velvet paroli and cloth piping.
- **Buttons**: Yellow, smooth.
- **Armament**: Sword with gilded hilt and nickel-plated steel scabbard (gilded fittings); knot and porte-épée like infantry officers.
- **Distinction**: Stars.

Artillery Ordnance Officials

a) Artillery Engineers

- **Hat & field cap**: Like intendance officials.
- **Tunic**: Dark brown, double row of buttons, scarlet collar, cuffs, and piping.
- **Trousers**: Blue-gray with scarlet piping.
- **Bluse**: Dark brown with scarlet paroli.
- **Overcoat**: Blue-gray with scarlet paroli and piping.
- **Buttons**: White, smooth.
- **Armament**: Like intendance, but with leather scabbard.
- **Distinction**: Stars.

b) Artillery Ordnance Officials

- Same as artillery engineers, but:
  - **Buttons**: Yellow.
  - No porte-épée.
  - **Distinction**: Rosettes.

Military Construction Officials

a) Construction Engineers

- **Hat & field cap**: Like intendance officials.
- **Tunic**: Light blue, double row of buttons, cherry-red velvet collar, cuffs, and piping.
- **Trousers**: Blue-gray with cherry-red velvet piping.
- **Bluse**: Light blue with cherry-red velvet paroli.
- **Overcoat**: Blue-gray with cherry-red velvet paroli and piping.
- **Buttons**: White, smooth.

- **Armament**: Like intendance, but with leather scabbard.
- **Distinction**: Stars.

b) Construction Foremen
- Same as construction engineers, but:
  - Cherry-red **cloth** (not velvet) trim.
  - No porte-épée.
  - **Buttons**: Yellow.
  - **Distinction**: Rosettes.

Technical Military Committee Officials
- Same as construction engineers, but:
  - **Buttons**: Yellow, smooth.
  - No porte-épée.
  - **Distinction**: Rosettes.

Military Audit Officials
- **Hat & field cap**: Like intendance officials.
- **Tunic**: Dark green, double row of buttons.
- **Bluse**: Dark green.
- **Trousers**: Blue-gray.
- **Overcoat**: Blue-gray with velvet collar.
- **Trim** (collar, cuffs, piping, paroli, etc.): Alizarin red.
- **Buttons**: White, smooth.
- **Sword**: Leather scabbard, no porte-épée.
- **Distinction**: Rosettes.

Military Treasury Officials
- Same as audit officials, but:
  - **Trim**: Rose red.

Commissariat Officials
- Same as audit officials, but:
  - **Trim**: Light blue.

Commissariat Assistant Deputies
- Same as commissariat officials, but:
  - Hat rosette, cap cord, and rosette in yellow silk.
  - **Distinction**: Like infantry officer deputies.

Military Registry Officials
- Same as audit officials, but:
  - **Trim**: Orange-yellow.

Military Medical Supply Officials
- Same as audit officials, but:
  - **Trim**: Crimson.

Military Construction Accounting Officials
- Same as audit officials, but:
  - **Trim**: Cherry red.

Technical Officials of the Military-Geographical Institute
- Same as audit officials, but:

- o **Trim**: Black velvet with scarlet piping.
- o **Buttons**: Yellow.

Military Instructors
- Same as audit officials, but:
  - o **Tunic**: Dark gray.
  - o **Bluse**: Dark blue.
  - o **Trim**: Scarlet.
  - o **Buttons**: Yellow, smooth.

Military Fencing Masters
- Same as military instructors, but:
  - o **Buttons**: White, smooth.

Military Veterinary Officials
- Same as audit officials, but:
  - o **Tunic & bluse**: Black.
  - o **Trim**: Crimson.
  - o **Buttons**: Yellow, smooth.
  - o **Sword**: Like intendance, but no porte-épée.

Military Forestry Officials
(For parades, same as audit officials with light blue trim.)
For regular forestry duty:
- **Tunic**: Light gray, single row of black horn buttons, grass-green collar, cuffs, shoulder rolls, and piping.
- **Breeches**: Light gray.
- **Armament**: Hunting hanger with gold knot, worn over the tunic.

Provosts
(Sergeant-major rank distinctions, but with silver braid.)
- **Hat**: With cock feather plume, like General Staff officers, but with yellow silk rosette and cord.
- **Cap**: Black, officer-style, black-yellow silk rosette and cord.
- **Tunic**: Blue-gray, single row of buttons, scarlet collar, cuffs, and piping.
- **Trousers**: Blue-gray with scarlet piping.
- **Bluse**: Blue-gray with scarlet paroli.
- **Overcoat**: Blue-gray with scarlet paroli and piping.
- **Buttons**: Yellow, smooth.
- **Armament**: Infantry officer saber, black-yellow silk knot and porte-épée.

Artisans and Technical Personnel

a) Senior Armorers (for Troops)
(Sergeant-major distinctions, but with silver braid.)
- **Hat**: Like provosts.
- **Cap**: Like provosts.
- **Tunic**: Dark blue, single row of buttons, crimson collar, cuffs, and piping.
- **Trousers**: Light blue.
- **Bluse**: Dark blue with crimson paroli.
- **Overcoat**: Blue-gray with crimson paroli and piping.
- **Buttons**: Yellow, smooth.
- **Armament**: Like provosts.

b) Workshop Foremen (for Uniform Administration)

(Sergeant-major distinctions, but with silver braid.)

- **Shako**: Like infantry cadet officer deputies.
- **Cap**: Like provosts.
- **Tunic**: Dark green, single row of buttons, russet collar, cuffs, and piping.
- **Trousers**: Blue-gray with russet piping.
- **Bluse**: Dark green with russet paroli.
- **Overcoat**: Blue-gray with russet paroli and piping.
- **Buttons**: Yellow, smooth.
- **Armament**: Like provosts.

c) Construction Foremen

(Sergeant-major distinctions, but with silver braid.)

- **Hat**: Like provosts.
- **Cap**: Like provosts.
- **Tunic**: Light blue, double row of buttons, cherry-red collar, cuffs, and piping.
- **Trousers**: Blue-gray with cherry-red piping.
- **Bluse**: Light blue with cherry-red paroli.
- **Overcoat**: Blue-gray with cherry-red paroli and piping.
- **Buttons**: Yellow, smooth.
- **Armament**: Like provosts.

Military Units Not Integrated into the Army
Imperial-Royal Gendarmerie
(14 commands.). pag. 36

Officers

- **Helmet**: Black, with a gilt double eagle and fittings.
- **Field cap**: Like infantry officers.
- **Tunic**: Steel-green, with two rows of buttons, crimson collar, cuffs, and piping; golden hanging cord for parades.
- **Trousers**: Blue-gray, with crimson piping.
- **Blouse**: Steel-green, with crimson collar patches.
- **Overcoat**: Blue-gray, with velvet collar, crimson patches, and piping.
- **Buttons**: Gilt, with numbers.
- **Armament**: Infantry officer's saber with gold pommel and golden porte-épée.

Enlisted Men

- **Helmet**: Black for parades, with yellow-metal double eagle and fittings; for service, a cork helmet with khaki cover and same fittings.
- **Field cap**: Steel-green, same style as officers (without storm band), rosette and cords of black-yellow silk; thin distinction cords: 3 for sergeants, 2 for leaders, 1 for gendarmes.
- **Tunic**: Steel-green, two rows of buttons, crimson collar, cuffs, piping, shoulder straps, and rolls; black-yellow hanging cord for parades.
- **Trousers**: Blue-gray, with crimson piping.
- **Blouse**: Steel-green, with shoulder straps and crimson collar patches.
- **Overcoat**: Blue-gray, with shoulder straps and crimson patches.

- **Buttons**: Yellow, with numbers.
- **Belt equipment**: Black.
- **Armament**: Repeating carbine with bayonet and gendarmerie enlisted saber; sergeants carry officer sabers like officer deputies.

Command Distinctions
- Buttons with numbers.

Accountants
Same as army accountants but with yellow numbered buttons.

Royal Hungarian (k.u.) Gendarmerie
(6 District Commands and one Hungarian-Croatian-Slavonian Gendarmerie Command)

Officers
- **Hat**: With cock feather plume, like rifle officers; emblem: Hungarian coat of arms.
- **Field cap**: Like infantry officers.
- **Tunic**: Steel-green, crimson collar, cuffs, and piping; collar and cuffs may have gold braiding.
- **Trousers**: Blue-gray, with crimson piping.
- **Blouse**: Steel-green, with gold braiding and metal buttons, plus crimson collar patches.
- **Overcoat**: Blue-gray, with velvet collar, crimson patches, and piping.
- **Buttons**: Smooth and gilt.
- **Armament**: Infantry officer's saber with gold pommel and golden porte-épée.

Foot Enlisted Men
- **Hat**: With cock feather plume, like rifle troops; emblem: Hungarian coat of arms.
- **Field cap**: Blue-gray, with visor and rosette.
- **Tunic**: Dark green, crimson collar, cuffs, and piping; collar and cuffs may have crimson braiding.
- **Winter/Summer blouse**: (Winter lined), steel-green, crimson patches and crimson Ispahan braiding, with metal buttons.
- **Trousers**: Blue-gray, with crimson piping.
- **Overcoat**: Blue-gray, with shoulder straps and crimson patches.
- **Buttons**: Yellow and smooth.
- **Belt equipment**: Black.
- **Armament**: Repeating carbine with bayonet and gendarmerie enlisted saber; sergeants carry sabers like officer deputies.

Mounted Enlisted Men
Same as foot troops, but with blue-gray tight riding breeches (leather-reinforced), crimson piping, high boots with spurs, cavalry saber, repeating carbine, and cavalry revolver.

Military Police Guard Corps

Enlisted Men
- **Czako**: Like infantry.
- **Cap**: Dark green, officer-style, with black-yellow wool rosette and cord.
- **Tunic**: Dark green, single row of buttons, crimson collar, cuffs, shoulder straps, and rolls.
- **Fur coat**: Dark green, same style as tunic.
- **Trousers**: Blue-gray, with crimson patches.
- **Overcoat**: Blue-gray, with shoulder straps and crimson patches.
- **Buttons**: Yellow and smooth.

- **Belt equipment**: Black.
- **Armament**: Rifle with bayonet and infantry enlisted saber with brass grip.
- **Mounted troops**: Same uniform as cavalry, with cavalry saber.

Officers
Same as infantry officers, matching their troops' colors, except for the cap.

Military Guard Corps for Civil Courts (Vienna)

Enlisted Men
- **Czako**: Like infantry.
- **Cap**: Like Police Guard Corps, with violet piping.
- **Tunic**: Dark green, single row of buttons, violet collar, cuffs, shoulder straps, and rolls.
- **Trousers**: Blue-gray, with violet piping.
- **Blouse**: With shoulder straps, dark green, violet patches.
- **Overcoat**: Blue-gray, with violet patches.
- **Buttons**: Yellow and smooth.
- **Belt equipment**: Black.
- **Armament**: Same as Police Guard Corps.

Officers
Same as infantry officers, matching their troops' colors, except for the cap.

Stud Farm Branch
Military Units of the Imperial and Royal State Stallion Depots

Officers
- **Czako**: With horsehair plume; field cap like artillery officers.
- **Tunic**: Dark brown, single row of buttons, crimson collar, cuffs, and piping; gold shoulder cord and hanging cord; matching fur coat.
- **Riding breeches**: Crimson, with high boots and spurs.
- **Dress trousers**: Blue-gray, with crimson piping.
- **Overcoat**: Dark brown, with velvet collar, crimson patches, and piping.
- **Buttons**: Yellow and smooth.
- **Armament**: Cavalry officer's saber with gold pommel and porte-épée.

Enlisted Men
- **Czako**: Like artillery.
- **Field cap**: Like cavalry.
- **Tunic**: Dark brown, single row of buttons, crimson collar and cuffs; matching fur coat.
- **Riding breeches**: Crimson, with high boots and sporns.
- **Overcoat**: Dark brown, with crimson patches.
- **Buttons**: Yellow and smooth.
- **Armament**: Cavalry enlisted saber.

Military Units of the Royal Hungarian Stud Farms

Officers
- **Czako**: Crimson, otherwise like hussar officers.
- **Field cap**: Like infantry officers.
- **Winter Attila**: Dark brown, with gold braiding and olives, black-trimmed.

- **Summer Attila**: Dark brown, with gold braiding and olives.
- **Riding breeches**: Crimson, tight, with gold braid like hussars; Csizmás (Hungarian boots) with sporns.
- **Dress trousers**: Blue-gray, with crimson piping.
- **Overcoat**: Dark brown, with velvet collar, crimson patches, and piping.
- **Buttons (olives)**: Yellow and smooth.
- **Armament**: Cavalry officer's saber with gold pommel and porte-épée.

Cadet Officer Deputies

Generally like officers (czako like enlisted men). Differences as per hussar cadet officer deputies.

Enlisted Men

- **Czako**: Crimson, otherwise like hussars.
- **Field cap**: Crimson, like dragoons.
- **Attila**: Dark brown, with black-yellow wool braiding.
- **Riding breeches**: Crimson, tight, with black-yellow wool braid like hussars; Csizmás with sporns.
- **Overcoat**: Dark brown, with crimson patches.
- **Buttons (olives)**: Yellow and smooth.
- **Armament**: Cavalry enlisted saber.

Imperial and Royal Austro-Hungarian Navy
Naval Officers
(Flag, Staff, and Senior Officers)

Gala Uniform (1a)

- **Hat**: Similar to that of engineering officers, without a plume. The left brim is slightly higher, with gold rosettes bearing "F.J.I." (Franz Joseph I). The braided gold cord extends from the front right edge of the brim, starting from a black cockade, arches toward the center of the lower brim, and is adorned with an embroidered anchor and crown.
- **Tunic**: Dark blue, with matching collar and cuffs, two rows of buttons, and gold epaulettes with bullion fringe.
- **Trousers**: Dark blue, with gold stripes.

Full Dress Uniform (Parade)

- **Hat**: As in Gala.
- **Frock Coat**: Dark blue, with folded collar, two rows of buttons, and gold epaulettes with bullion fringe on the shoulders.
- **Neckcloth**: Black silk.
- **Vest**: Dark blue, single row of buttons.
- **Trousers**: Dark blue, without gold stripes.
- **Summer Trousers**: White.
- **Overcoat**: Dark blue, with velvet collar.

Service Dress (Less Formal)

Same as Full Dress, but without epaulettes.

Everyday Uniform

- **Navy Cap**: Dark blue, with a large rounded top, downward-curved visor, black moiré band with rank braid, a gold cord as a chinstrap, and an embroidered emblem (gold "F.J.I." over an upright anchor, surrounded by laurel branches and topped by the imperial crown). In summer, a white cover may be used.
- **Frock Coat**: As in parade dress, but without epaulettes (only gold epaulette loops).
- **Jacket**: Dark blue, with two rows of buttons (alternative to the frock coat).
- **Neckcloth, Trousers, Summer Trousers, and Overcoat**: As in Full Dress.
- **Raincoat**: Dark blue, similar to the overcoat but with a rain collar extending to the hips.

White (Tropical) Uniform

Worn in hot climates and appropriate conditions (except Gala):

- **Tropical Helmet**: White, with imperial crown and "A.H." monogram (like the cap).
- **Cap**: With white cover.
- **Jacket**: White, single row of buttons, 6 cm wide dark blue shoulder straps edged with gold cord, displaying rank insignia as on the frock coat.
- **Summer Trousers**: White.

For All Uniform Types

- **Buttons**: Gilt, decorated with a crown and anchor.
- **Sidearm**: Naval officer's saber, with gilt basket hilt, leather scabbard with gilt fittings, gilt pommel, and gold porte-épée.

Notes on Rank Insignia

- **Cap Braid**:
  - Junior Officers: One braid.
  - Staff Officers: Two braids.
  - Flag Officers: Three braids.
- **Epaulettes**:
  - Flag Officers: Gold shoulder plate with embroidered imperial crown and large silver rank stars.
  - Staff/Senior Officers: Smaller crown with the naval emblem (fouled anchor) in gold.
- **Bullion Fringe**:
  - Flag/Staff Officers: 7 mm thick.
  - Junior Officers: 3 mm thick.
- **Trouser Stripes (Gala)**:
  - Flag Officers: Two 2.6 cm gold stripes.
  - Staff Officers: One 3.2 cm stripe.
  - Junior Officers: One 2 cm stripe.
- **Sleeve Distinctions**:
  - **Flag Officers**: Wide gold bands + 1–3 braids (top one with "Elliot's eye") + crown.
  - **Staff Officers**: Narrower gold band + 1–3 braids (top with Elliot's eye).
  - **Junior Officers**: 2–3 braids (top with Elliot's eye).
  - On white jackets, insignia are placed horizontally on shoulder straps.

Elliot's Eye: A 3.5 cm upward loop, denoting combatant status (absent for doctors/officials).

Naval Cadets

Similar to officers but with distinctions:

- **Hat Rosettes**: Yellow silk instead of gold.
- **Cap**: No rank braid; chinstrap of black silk cord.
- **Epaulettes**: Without bullion fringe.
- **Gala Trousers**: No gold stripes.
- **Sidearm**: Officer-style saber, but with black leather pommel and yellow silk porte-épée.
- **Rank Insignia**:
  - **2nd Class**: 9 cm gold braid with Elliot's eye on cuff.
  - **1st Class**: Same, but encircling the entire cuff.

Petty Officers & Senior NCOs

(Boatswains, Helmsmen, Machinists, etc.)

- **Cap**: Dark blue (like officers'), with yellow-metal rosettes (anchor + "F.J.I." + crown).
- **Frock Coat**: Dark blue, folded collar, shoulder straps for parades.
- **Trousers**: Dark blue.
- **Summer Trousers**: White.
- **Jacket**: Dark blue, folded collar.
- **Overcoat**: Dark blue.
- **Buttons**: Yellow, with anchor.
- **Sidearm**: Naval saber, black leather fittings, black-yellow wool porte-épée.

Tropical Uniform

- White helmet or cap with white cover.
- White jacket with dark blue shoulder straps (rank insignia as on frock coat).
- White summer trousers.

Rank Insignia

- **Old System**: Yellow silk braids (9 mm wide) around cuffs:
  - Chief Boatswain: 3 braids.
  - Boatswain: 2 braids.
  - Junior Boatswain: 1 braid.
- **New System**: Gold braids (1.3 cm wide, 11 cm long) on cuff edges + small button:
  - Chief: 3 braids.
  - Boatswain: 2 braids.

Seamen & Junior NCOs
Hot Weather

- **Cap**: Dark blue, no visor, black silk band with ship name (e.g., "Lissa"). Enlisted wear yellow rosette ("F.J.I."); NCOs add a small crown.
- **Tropical Helmet**: Optional.
- **Shirt**: White calico, blue collar with three white stripes.
- **Undershirt**: Blue/white striped wool.
- **Trousers**: White.

Cold Weather

- **Cap**: As above.
- **Wool Shirt**: Dark blue, with rank insignia on sleeves.
- **Jacket**: White, with detachable blue collar.
- **Undershirt**: White.
- **Neckcloth**: Black.
- **Trousers**: Dark blue.
- **Overcoat**: Dark blue, hip-length.
- **Buttons**: Yellow, with anchor.
- **Weapons**: Saber, rifle, bayonet, or revolver.

Rank Insignia

White stars on the blue collar (with three white edge stripes).

Naval Band (Musik-Mannschaft)

- **Cap**: Dark blue, like senior NCOs (with the imperial crown, but only for NCOs).
- **Tunic**: Dark blue, with matching cuffs and collar; the collar bears a yellow-metal lyre. Shoulder straps are covered with triple-braided black-yellow silk cord.
- **Trousers**: Dark blue.

- **Summer Trousers**: White.
- **Blouse**: Dark blue, with a lyre insignia.
- **Overcoat**: Dark blue.
- **Winter/Summer Undershirts**: Same as sailors.
- **Belt Equipment**: Black.
- **Buttons**: Yellow, with an anchor.
- **Sidearm**: Naval saber.

Naval Academy Cadets

Parade Uniform
- **Cap**: Like naval cadets.
- **Spencer (Jacket)**: Dark blue, with folded collar; rank distinction of one or two gold braids with a small button at the collar ends.
- **Neckcloth**: Like naval cadets.
- **Trousers**: Dark blue.
- **Summer Trousers**: White.
- **Overcoat**: Dark blue.

Bord & Daily Wear
- **Sailor Cap**: Like enlisted sailors.
- **Shirt**: Blue linen or dark blue wool, like sailors.
- **Trousers**: Dark blue (summer: blue linen).
- **Buttons**: Yellow, with an anchor.
- **Sidearm**: Dagger in a black leather sheath, carried on a braided leather belt with a black-yellow silk porte-épée.

Naval Chaplains & Auditors
(Generally the same as the Army.)

Naval Medical Officers
- **Hat & Cap**: Like naval officers, but the cap emblem is on a black background.
- **Frock Coat**: Like officers', with black velvet cuffs.
- **Neckcloth**: Like officers'.
- **Tunic**: Like officers', with black velvet collar and cuffs; shoulder loops edged in black and gold.
- **Trousers**: Like officers', with or without gold stripes.
- **Summer Trousers/Jackets/Overcoat**: As for officers.
- **Buttons & Sidearm**: Like officers.

Distinctions
- **Epaulettes**: Silver shoulder plates (instead of gold) with a gold Aesculapius staff (instead of the naval emblem).
- **Rank Braid**: Like officers, but with black gaps between braids; no Elliot's eye.
  - *Surgeon General*: Wears a star above braids instead of a crown.

Naval Officials
Technical Officials
- **Hat**: Like officers, but rosettes feature an eagle (not "F.J.I."); hat cord made of double gold braid.
- **Cap**: Like officers', but with a silver-embroidered "A.H." monogram and anchor on cherry-red backing.
- **Frock Coat**: Like officers', with cherry-red velvet cuffs.

- **Tunic**: Like officers', with cherry-red velvet collar and cuffs.
- **Trousers/Summer Wear/Jackets/Overcoat**: As for officers.
- **Buttons**: Like officers.
- **Sidearm**: Sword with gilt pommel and gold porte-épée (but silver button and band).

Rank Insignia
- **Epaulettes**: Silver plates with cherry-red silk-edged rims.
- **Sleeve Braids**: Like officers, but gaps are cherry-red; no Elliot's eye.
  - *Class V Officials*: Wear a rosette instead of a crown.
- **Exceptions**:
  - *Machinery Directors*: Dove-gray (instead of cherry-red).
  - *Workshop Foremen*: Scarlet.

Commissariat Officials
Same as technical officials, but with light blue velvet (for emblems, cuffs, and collar trim).

Hydrographic & Educational Officials
Same as technical officials, but with dark blue velvet distinctions.

Naval Bandmaster (Marine-Kapellmeister)
- **Hat**: Like naval cadets, but with silver cord and rosettes.
- **Cap**: Like cadets', but with a gold-embroidered lyre (replacing "F.J.I.") under the crown; moiré band has silver braid.
- **Uniforms**: Like cadets', but with:
  - Gold-embroidered lyres on collar ends.
  - Shoulder straps of braided silver cord.
  - Silver-embroidered lyre on white jacket's shoulder straps.
- **Sidearm**: Like cadets', but with silver pommel and red/silver porte-épée.

Officers' Servants
Same as enlisted sailors, but with a red chevron on the right sleeve as a service badge.

Note: The uniform illustrated in the color plates is no longer in use.

LANDWEHR INFANTRY
(36 Regiments, No. 1–37, excluding Regiment No. 4.)

Officers
- **Hat**, with cock's feather plume and field cap, like officers of the Feldjäger battalions.
- **Tunic**, pike-gray, with a single row of buttons, grass-green collar, cuffs, and piping.
- **Trousers**, blue-gray, with grass-green piping; when mounted, configured as riding breeches.
- **Blouse**, pike-gray, with grass-green collar patches.
- **Overcoat**, with velvet collar, blue-gray, with grass-green collar patches and piping.
- **Buttons**, silver-plated with regimental numbers in Arabic numerals.
- **Armament**: Infantry officer's sabre with gold pommel and gold porte-épée.

Cadet Officer Deputies
- **Hat**, with cock's feather plume like officers, but with green silk hat cord instead of gold.
- All else generally like officers, except cap cords and rosettes, as well as sabre pommel and porte-épée, are of black-and-yellow silk.
- On the tunic and blouse, shoulder straps like enlisted men; on the overcoat, also piped shoulder straps, and the collar is of cloth.

Enlisted Men

- **Hat**, with feather plume like Jäger troops.
- **Field cap**, blue-gray with a visor and metal rosette marked *F.J.1*.
- **Tunic**, pike-gray, with grass-green collar, cuffs, and shoulder straps with raised seams; regimental numbers in Arabic numerals (Alpacca metal) on shoulder straps.
- **Blouse**, pike-gray with grass-green collar patches and shoulder straps (latter with regimental numbers in Alpacca).
- **Trousers**, blue-gray with grass-green piping.
- **Overcoat**, with shoulder straps, blue-gray with grass-green collar patches.
- **Buttons**, white and smooth.
- **Equipment**, black, with a yellow buckle on the waist belt.
- **Armament**, like regular army infantry.
- **Regimental distinctions**: For officers, buttons with numbers; for enlisted men, Arabic numerals on Alpacca shoulder straps; for both, the regimental number in Arabic numerals on the hat badge (for officers also on the cap badge).

Regimental and battalion buglers wear riding breeches; if serving longer, they may also wear trousers off-duty.

Note

In 1907, a partial re-uniforming was introduced, to be implemented gradually.

a) For Officers (except those in local postings)

- **Trousers**, pike-gray with grass-green piping and double stripes (alongside the existing blue-gray ones).
- **Overcoat**, in a yet-to-be-determined shade (likely mouse-gray), but only at a later date.

b) For Enlisted Men

- **Field cap**, pike-gray, otherwise as before.
- **Trousers**, pike-gray with grass-green piping.
- **Overcoat**, likely mouse-gray with grass-green collar patches—but only later.

c) For Cadet Officer Deputies

- Trousers like enlisted men, not like officers.

Landesschützen (Tyrol and Vorarlberg)

(2 Regiments, No. I–II, and Landwehr Infantry Regiment No. 4)

These mountain troops, previously uniformed like Landwehr infantry, received new regulations in 1907. Enlisted men's parade items (hat, tunic) were abolished entirely; officers retained some parade items (hat, tunic, trousers) only for peacetime wear outside the unit. Otherwise, the new **field uniform** was prescribed for parades, marches, and certain duties.

Officers

- **Parade (peacetime, outside unit)**:
    - **Hat**, with cock's feather plume (Tyrolean eagle on badge).
    - **Tunic**, pike-gray, two rows of buttons, grass-green distinctions; silver edelweiss embroidery on collar.
    - **Trousers**, pike-gray with grass-green piping and double stripes.
    - **Armament**: Officer's sabre with gold fittings; field sash for parades.
- **Field Uniform (also for marches/parades with troops)**:
    - **Field cap**, pike-gray, with imperial cypher and crown in gilt metal.
    - **Blouse**, pike-gray, with grass-green distinctions and silver edelweiss on collar.
    - **Knee breeches**, pike-gray with grass-green piping, worn with wool gaiters.
    - **Riding breeches** for mounted troops.
    - **Overcoat**, currently blue-gray (later likely mouse-gray).
    - **Armament**: Short officer's sabre with gold porte-épée, worn on a brown leather belt.

Enlisted Men

- **Field cap**, pike-gray, with gamecock feather for parades.
- **Blouse**, pike-gray, with grass-green distinctions and Alpacca edelweiss on collar.
- **Knee breeches**, pike-gray, with wool gaiters.
- **Overcoat**, currently blue-gray (later mouse-gray).
- **Armament**: Repeating rifle with bayonet; NCOs and buglers carry short sabres.
- **Alpine gear**: Ice axe, climbing poles, crampons, and field blanket.

Mounted Landwehr Troops

Landwehr Uhlans (6 Regiments, No. 1–6)
Like regular army Uhlans, but with white czapka rosettes bearing regimental numbers.

Mounted Tyrolean Landesschützen (2 Squadrons)
- **Officers**: Like Landwehr infantry but with Tyrolean eagle on hat badge.
- **Enlisted**: Similar, with pike-gray tunics and riding breeches.

Mounted Dalmatian Landesschützen (2 Squadrons)
Like Tyrolean mounted troops but with imperial eagle insignia (no fur coats for enlisted).

Other Units
- **Landwehr Artillery (8 regiments)**: Initially uniformed like regular artillery.
- **Landwehr Supply Officers**: Like army equivalents but with yellow buttons.
- **Landwehr District Sergeants**: Like officer deputies but with silver braid.
- **Landwehr Cadet School**: Uniforms like infantry/cavalry but with imperial eagle insignia.
- **One-Year Volunteer Schools**: Trainees wear their unit's uniform with yellow-black braid on sleeves.

Administrative & Technical Personnel
- **Clergy, Doctors, Auditors, Accountants, etc.**: Like their army counterparts but with white/gilt buttons.
- **Engineers, Armorers, Veterinary Staff**: Varied distinctions, mostly with white/yellow buttons.

Royal Hungarian Landwehr (Honvéd)
Honvéd Infantry
(28 Regiments, No. 1–28.)

Officers
- **Czako (Shako)**: Dark blue, with visor, gilded rosette featuring the Hungarian crown and initials *"l.f.J."*; front plate displays the gilded Hungarian coat of arms with the motto *"For King and Fatherland"* (in Hungarian or Croatian).
- **Field cap**: Like infantry officers of the regular army.
- **Dolman (Tunic)**: Dark blue, double row of buttons, gold braiding with red threading on collar and cuffs.
- **Trousers**: Light blue.
- **Dress trousers**: Blue-gray with crimson piping.
- **Blouse**: Dark blue with crimson collar patches.
- **Overcoat**: Blue-gray with velvet collar, crimson collar patches and piping.
- **Buttons**: Gilded and smooth.
- **Armament**: Like regular army infantry officers.

Cadet Officer Deputies
- **Czako**: Like enlisted men; all else as officers, but with cherry-red braiding (instead of gold), yellow (red-threaded) silk cords/rosettes, and cloth collar on the overcoat.

Enlisted Men
- **Czako**: Dark blue, with visor, yellow-metal rosette (Hungarian crown and *"l.f.J."*), front plate with

- **Field cap**: Dark blue, with visor and rosette ("*I.f.J.*"); regimental number in red cloth on the right side.
- **Dolman**: Dark blue, with cherry-red braiding on collar and cuffs, raised shoulder seams.
- **Legwear**: Tight light-blue trousers with cherry-red braiding.
- **Blouse**: Dark blue with crimson collar patches.
- **Overcoat**: Blue-gray with crimson collar patches.
- **Buttons**: Yellow and smooth.
- **Equipment**: Black leather with waist belt buckle bearing the Hungarian coat of arms.
- **Armament**: Like regular army infantry.
- **Regimental distinctions**: Enlisted men wear regimental numbers on field caps.

Honvéd Staff (District) Sergeants

Like officer deputies but with light-blue distinctions on dolman/blouse, dark-gray trousers, and silver braid for sergeant rank.

Honvéd Hussars
(10 Regiments, No. 1–10.)

Officers

- **Czako**: Like Honvéd infantry officers but in regimental colors, with gold-and-red "*Vitéz Kötés*" (braided cord) and white upright horsehair plume.
- **Attila (Jacket)**: Dark blue, gold braiding with red threading, gold shoulder cords.
- **Pelisse**: Dark blue with white fur trim, gold braiding, and shoulder cords.
- **Riding breeches**: Crimson with gold braiding; worn with "*csizma*" boots and spurs.
- **Dress trousers**: Blue-gray with crimson piping.
- **Blouse**: Dark blue with gold braiding on collar, cuffs, and chest.
- **Overcoat**: Dark brown with crimson collar patches/piping.
- **Buttons**: Gilded and conical.
- **Armament**: Like dragoon officers of the regular army.

Cadet Officer Deputies

Like officers but with cherry-red braiding (instead of gold) and cloth overcoat collar.

Enlisted Men

- **Czako**: Like Honvéd infantry but with regimental colors, cherry-red "*Vitéz Kötés*", and white horsehair plume.
- **Field cap**: Crimson, with regimental number in yellow cloth.
- **Pelisse**: Dark blue with white fur trim and cherry-red braiding.
- **Riding breeches**: Crimson with cherry-red braiding.
- **Blouse**: Dark blue with cherry-red braiding.
- **Overcoat**: Dark brown with crimson collar patches.
- **Buttons**: Yellow and conical.
- **Armament**: Like regular army dragoons.

Regimental Czako Colors:

1. Gray | 2. Light blue | 3. White | 4. Black | 5. Dark blue | 6. Green | 7–10. Crimson

Honvéd Educational Institutions

- **Cadet Schools**: Uniforms like Honvéd infantry officer deputies, but with rifles/bayonets like enlisted men.
- **Honvéd Oberrealschule**: Cadet uniform with additional yellow silk arm stripes.
- **Ludovica Academy**: Gold arm stripes (similar to army academies).

Support Personnel

- **Auditors**: Black dolman/blouse, blue-gray trousers with crimson piping.

- **Doctors**: Light-blue dolman with black velvet (red-piped) collar/cuffs; blue-gray trousers.
- **Administrative Officers**: Dark-green dolman, light-blue distinctions.
- **Veterinarians**: Black dolman with cherry-red velvet/gold braid; blue-gray trousers.

Bosnian-Herzegovinian Troops
Infantry (4 Regiments, No. 1–4)

- **Officers**:
  - **Fez** (for Muslims) or **Czako** (non-Muslims); light-blue tunic with madder-red distinctions.
- **Enlisted**:
  - **Fez** with dark-blue tassel; light-blue uniforms with madder-red piping; knee breeches with gaiters.

Jäger Battalion
- Pike-gray uniforms with grass-green distinctions; yellow buttons.

Gendarmerie
- Similar to Austrian *Landesgendarmerie* but with fez (Muslims), red sleeve braiding, and yellow buttons.

Royal Hungarian Landwehr (Honvéd)
Honvéd Infantry
(28 Regiments, No. 1–28.)

Officers
- **Czako (Shako)**: Dark blue, with visor, gilded rosette featuring the Hungarian crown and initials *"l.f.J."*; front plate displays the gilded Hungarian coat of arms with the motto *"For King and Fatherland"* (in Hungarian or Croatian).
- **Field cap**: Like infantry officers of the regular army.
- **Dolman (Tunic)**: Dark blue, double row of buttons, gold braiding with red threading on collar and cuffs.
- **Trousers**: Light blue.
- **Dress trousers**: Blue-gray with crimson piping.
- **Blouse**: Dark blue with crimson collar patches.
- **Overcoat**: Blue-gray with velvet collar, crimson collar patches and piping.
- **Buttons**: Gilded and smooth.
- **Armament**: Like regular army infantry officers.

Cadet Officer Deputies
- **Czako**: Like enlisted men; all else as officers, but with cherry-red braiding (instead of gold), yellow (red-threaded) silk cords/rosettes, and cloth collar on the overcoat.

Enlisted Men
- **Czako**: Dark blue, with visor, yellow-metal rosette (Hungarian crown and *"l.f.J."*), front plate with yellow-metal coat of arms and motto.
- **Field cap**: Dark blue, with visor and rosette (*"l.f.J."*); regimental number in red cloth on the right side.
- **Dolman**: Dark blue, with cherry-red braiding on collar and cuffs, raised shoulder seams.
- **Legwear**: Tight light-blue trousers with cherry-red braiding.
- **Blouse**: Dark blue with crimson collar patches.
- **Overcoat**: Blue-gray with crimson collar patches.
- **Buttons**: Yellow and smooth.
- **Equipment**: Black leather with waist belt buckle bearing the Hungarian coat of arms.
- **Armament**: Like regular army infantry.
- **Regimental distinctions**: Enlisted men wear regimental numbers on field caps.

Honvéd Staff (District) Sergeants
Like officer deputies but with light-blue distinctions on dolman/blouse, dark-gray trousers, and silver braid for sergeant rank.

Honvéd Hussars
(10 Regiments, No. 1–10.)
Officers

- **Czako**: Like Honvéd infantry officers but in regimental colors, with gold-and-red *"Vitéz Kötés"* (braided cord) and white upright horsehair plume.
- **Attila (Jacket)**: Dark blue, gold braiding with red threading, gold shoulder cords.
- **Pelisse**: Dark blue with white fur trim, gold braiding, and shoulder cords.
- **Riding breeches**: Crimson with gold braiding; worn with *"csizma"* boots and spurs.
- **Dress trousers**: Blue-gray with crimson piping.
- **Blouse**: Dark blue with gold braiding on collar, cuffs, and chest.
- **Overcoat**: Dark brown with crimson collar patches/piping.
- **Buttons**: Gilded and conical.
- **Armament**: Like dragoon officers of the regular army.

Cadet Officer Deputies
Like officers but with cherry-red braiding (instead of gold) and cloth overcoat collar.

Enlisted Men

- **Czako**: Like Honvéd infantry but with regimental colors, cherry-red *"Vitéz Kötés"*, and white horsehair plume.
- **Field cap**: Crimson, with regimental number in yellow cloth.
- **Pelisse**: Dark blue with white fur trim and cherry-red braiding.
- **Riding breeches**: Crimson with cherry-red braiding.
- **Blouse**: Dark blue with cherry-red braiding.
- **Overcoat**: Dark brown with crimson collar patches.
- **Buttons**: Yellow and conical.
- **Armament**: Like regular army dragoons.

Regimental Czako Colors:
1. Gray | 2. Light blue | 3. White | 4. Black | 5. Dark blue | 6. Green | 7–10. Crimson

Honvéd Educational Institutions

- **Cadet Schools**: Uniforms like Honvéd infantry officer deputies, but with rifles/bayonets like enlisted men.
- **Honvéd Oberrealschule**: Cadet uniform with additional yellow silk arm stripes.
- **Ludovica Academy**: Gold arm stripes (similar to army academies).

Support Personnel

- **Auditors**: Black dolman/blouse, blue-gray trousers with crimson piping.
- **Doctors**: Light-blue dolman with black velvet (red-piped) collar/cuffs; blue-gray trousers.
- **Administrative Officers**: Dark-green dolman, light-blue distinctions.
- **Veterinarians**: Black dolman with cherry-red velvet/gold braid; blue-gray trousers.

Bosnian-Herzegovinian Troops
Infantry (4 Regiments, No. 1–4)
Officers

- **Czako** (for non-Muslims): As per officers of the Imperial and Royal (k.u.k.) Infantry.
- **Fez** (for Muslims): Crimson red, with dark blue silk tassel.
- **Field cap**: As per infantry officers of the army (only permitted to be worn outside drill and formation).
- **Tunic**: Light blue, with a single row of buttons, alizarin-red collar, cuffs, and piping.
- **Trousers**: Light blue.
- **Walking-out trousers**: Blue-gray, with scarlet piping.
- **Blouse**: Light blue, with alizarin-red collar patches.

- **Overcoat**: Blue-gray, with velvet collar, alizarin-red collar patches, and piping.
- **Buttons**: Gilded, with regimental numbers.
- **Armament**: Same as infantry officers of the army.

Officer Deputies
Generally the same as officers, with the exceptions mentioned for the k.u.k. Infantry.

Enlisted Men
- **Fez**: Crimson red, with dark blue woolen tassel.
- **Tunic**: Light blue, with alizarin-red collar, cuffs, shoulder rolls, and shoulder straps.
- **Knee breeches**: Light blue, wide to the knee, tightly gaitered over the calves.
- **Blouse**: With shoulder straps, light blue, with alizarin-red collar patches.
- **Overcoat**: With shoulder straps, blue-gray, with alizarin-red collar patches.
- **Buttons**: Yellow, with regimental numbers.
- **Leather gear**: Black.
- **Armament**: Same as infantry enlisted men of the army.

Riflemen (Jäger) (1 Battalion.)

Same as Bosnian infantry, but the uniform is pike-gray, with grass-green distinctions and smooth yellow buttons.

Train Troops
(4 detachments, assigned to the army's train units.)

Enlisted Men
- **Fez**: Crimson red, with dark blue woolen tassel.
- Otherwise, same as enlisted men of the army's train troops.

Gendarmerie Corps for Bosnia and Herzegovina

Officers
All items as per officers of the Imperial Royal (k.k.) State Gendarmerie, but with smooth gilded buttons, no helmet—instead, a hat with a plume, and gold cords on the blouse sleeves.

Enlisted Men
- **Field cap**: Blue-gray, with a visor, bearing the highest monogram (F.J.I.) in yellow metal (for sergeants, same as k.k. Gendarmerie).
- **Fez** (for Muslims): Crimson red, without tassel, with the highest monogram as on the field cap.
- All other items as per enlisted men of the k.k. State Gendarmerie, but with red cord decoration on the blouse sleeves and smooth yellow buttons. Mounted gendarmes wear a blouse-like fur jacket and riding breeches instead of the blouse, no helmet or sword knot, and in service, knee breeches like those of the Bosnian-Herzegovinian infantry.

Military Boys' Boarding School (in Sarajevo.)

Cadets
- **Fez**: Crimson red, with dark blue tassel.
- **Field cap** (for non-Muslims): Crimson red, with visor and rosette.
- **Tunic**: Dark blue, with scarlet collar, cuffs, shoulder straps, shoulder rolls, and piping.
- **Trousers**: Blue-gray, with scarlet stripes for parades, otherwise plain.
- **Blouse**: Dark blue, with scarlet collar patches.
- **Overcoat**: Blue-gray, with scarlet collar patches.
- **Rank insignia**: Same as cadets of military secondary schools.
- **No armament**.

Military Imam (Muslim Chaplain)
- **Fez**: Crimson red, with white turban cloth (saruk) and black silk tassel.
- **Outer garment (Dzuke)**: A knee-length cloth coat, dark blue, with alizarin-red collar and cuffs, the latter adorned with three gold braids.
- **Waist sash (Pas)**: A red shawl wrapped around the waist.
- **Trousers**: Dark blue, wide, tapering tightly toward the shoes.

LANDSTURM
(In the Austrian half of the empire.)

Same as the Landwehr Infantry (Landesschützen), but enlisted men have no hat or tunic. Instead, their blouses have simple embroidered numeral loops on the shoulder straps (e.g., *1/31* = 1st Battalion of the 31st Landsturm District). Non-uniformed Landsturm members wear an armband with the corresponding number.

LANDSTURM
(in Hungary.)

Like the Honvéd infantry, but the personnel have no *czakos* (Hungarian military hats) or *attila* (Hungarian jackets). Landsturm members not in military uniform wear an armband as a military insignia.

Officials of the Red Cross Society at Field Medical Establishments

- **Hat**: Similar to that of Jäger officers, with an eagle emblem and a white rooster-feather plume.
- **Sash**: Like officers', with a small eagle and red cross.
- **Tunic**: Black, with collar, cuffs, and piping of scarlet velvet, a white breast panel with a scarlet Geneva Cross.
- **Trousers (Breeches)**: Blue-gray, with scarlet cloth piping.
- **Blouse**: Black, with scarlet velvet piping.
- **Overcoat**: Blue-gray, with a velvet collar and scarlet velvet piping.
- **Buttons**: Gilt, with an eagle and Geneva Cross.
- **Armament**: Like infantry officers, with the sabre hanger worn over the coat; all gold elements are interwoven with red.
- **Distinctions**: Rosettes like those of military officials.

Imperial-Royal Austrian Volunteer Automobile Corps
(Not included in the color illustrations.)

- **Automobile Cap**: Blue with the Imperial Crown and winged wheel.
- **Coat**: Blouse-style, blue with gray cuffs, bearing the Imperial Crown, yellow buttons, and shoulder straps.
- **Breeches**: Gray (for field uniform only), with yellow gaiters and laced shoes.
- **Long Trousers**: Blue with gray stripes (for dress uniform only).
- **Gray Overcoat**: (Officer's cut).
- **Yellow Waistbelt**: With a cartridge pouch, revolver in a yellow holster carried on a strap over the right shoulder.
- **Dress Sword**: For the dress uniform.

<u>Description of Insignia</u>
Insignia for Various Service Categories

Armband Insignia:

- **For Landsturm**: Worn on the left upper arm by non-uniformed personnel (e.g., Landsturm labor units). These armbands have white stitched numbers (e.g., *1/31 L St.*).
  - Austrian lands: Yellow with black central stripes.
  - Tyrol: Green and white.
  - Hungary: Green, white, and red.
- **Medical Personnel** (doctors, Red Cross delegates, stretcher-bearers, etc.): White cloth with a red cross, worn on the left upper arm of the outermost garment.
- **Senior Staff Wagonmasters**: Black cloth with a gilt Imperial double eagle and gold braid edging (like cadet distinction braid).
- **Staff Wagonmasters**: Imperial-yellow cloth with a black-lacquered Imperial double eagle.

- **Wagonmasters**: Imperial-yellow cloth with stitched numbers and abbreviated unit designation (e.g., *102. I.-R.* for *102nd Infantry Regiment*).
- **Staff Troops**: Yellow wool with a central black stripe, worn on the right upper arm.
- **Civilians** (e.g., sutlers, servants, and carters): Same armband with the unit number in white cloth.
- **Railway Service**: Yellow cloth with a black winged wheel.
- **Telegraphists**: Yellow cloth with a black "T."

Sleeve Insignia
(Uniform of the unit.)

- **One-Year Volunteers**: 1 cm wide yellow silk arm stripes with black central stripes on both sleeves.
- **Honvéd Realschule Cadets**: Same, but with red instead of black stripes.
- **Senior Academicians**: Same golden arm stripes; also for Honvéd Ludovica Academy cadets.
- **Armorers, Farriers, Squadron Harness-Makers**: Yellow corporal's *czako* braid on both sleeves.
- **Long-Service Volunteer NCOs**: On the left sleeve, an upward-angled gilt braid (1.3 cm wide, similar to cadet braid); after 3 years of service, an additional 1.6 mm gilt braid.
- **Officers' Servants and Grooms**: On the right sleeve, an upward-angled 1 cm wide crimson braid.

Sleeve Insignia for Naval Specializations

These insignia, representing emblems of the naval forces, are:

- For the frock coats and jackets of senior non-commissioned officers: **embroidered in gold**.
- For the deck shirts of the remaining crew: **woven in imperial-yellow, wood-brown shaded sheep's wool**, while on white calico shirts, they are **printed in black aniline dye**.

They are worn on the **left upper arm** of the specified garments. Exceptions to this apply to **medical service insignia** and **quarters insignia**, which are discussed separately.

These emblems are as follows:

a) **Deck Service**: A **vertical anchor with a coiled rope** – worn from *Oberbootsmann* (Chief Boatswain) down to *Quartiermeister* (Quartermaster), while *Marsgast* (Topman) and *Matrosen 1. Klasse* (Seamen 1st Class) wear it **without the Imperial Crown**.

b) **Steering Service**: A **vertical anchor with a steering wheel** – worn from *Obersteuermann* (Chief Helmsman) down to *Steuer-Quartiermeister* (Helmsman Quartermaster), while *Steuergast* (Helmsman's Mate) and *Steuer-Matrose* (Helmsman Seaman) wear it **without the Imperial Crown**.

c) **Engine Service**: A **horizontal propeller** – worn from *Obermaschinenwärter* (Chief Machinist) down to *Maschinen-Quartiermeister* (Machinist Quartermaster), while *Maschinengast* (Machinist's Mate), *Oberheizer* (Chief Stoker), and *Heizer* (Stoker) wear it **without the Imperial Crown**.

d) **Armament Service**: **Two crossed sabers** – worn from *Waffenmeister* (Armorer) down to *Waffen-Quartiermeister* (Armorer Quartermaster), while *Waffgast* (Armorer's Mate) wears it **without the Imperial Crown**.

e) **Artillery Service**: A **vertical anchor with a coiled rope** –
- For the *Artillerie-Instruktor* (Artillery Instructor): with a **horizontal cannon barrel and Imperial Crown**.
- For *Vormeister II. und I. Klasse* (Gun Captains 2nd and 1st Class): with **two crossed cannon barrels**.
- For *Matrosenkanoniere* (Seaman Gunners): with a **single horizontal cannon barrel**.

f) **Medical Service**: A **vertical cross in scarlet sheep's wool**, worn by *Ober-Krankenwärter* (Senior Medical Orderly) and *Krankenwärter* (Medical Orderly).

g) **Quarters Insignia**: Stripes (1¼ cm wide, 12 cm long) –
- For deck shirts: in **scarlet cloth**.
- For white calico shirts: in **dark blue calico**, sewn near the sleeve seam.
  - For the **starboard section**: on the **right sleeve**.
  - For the **port section**: on the **left sleeve**.
- Crew of the **1st and 2nd quarters**: **one stripe each**.
- Crew of the **3rd and 4th quarters**: **two stripes each**.

Additional Insignia (not illustrated in color plates):

- **Machine Gun Service:** As in (e), but with a **star below**.
- **Torpedo Service:** An **anchor with 1 or 2 burning grenades**.
- **Mine Service:** An **anchor with 1 or 2 mine anchors**.
- **Laborers:** Two **crossed pickaxes**.
- **Provision/Kitchen Service:** Two **crossed grain ears**.
- **For all NCOs:** The **Imperial Crown** is added above.

Rank Distinctions

The primary **rank distinction insignia** for personnel of the **land forces** are displayed on the **collars of tunics**, *attilas*, *uhlankas*, **blouses**, etc., and consist of the following:

a) Officers (including military auditors, doctors, supply officers, paymasters, and certain officials):

- **General Officers:** Gold embroidery (or gold braid) with silver-embroidered stars; additionally, **gold embroidery or a 5 cm wide gold braid on the cuff**.
- **Staff Officers:** Gold or silver braid (matching buttons) and **silver or gold-embroidered stars** (opposite button color); additionally, a **3.3 cm wide gold or silver braid on cuffs**.
- **Subaltern Officers:** Gold or silver-embroidered stars (matching buttons).

b) Non-Commissioned Officers and Enlisted Men:

- **Cadet Officer Deputies and Equivalents:** Gold braid with silver-plated stars.
- **Other Cadets:** Gold braid with white celluloid stars (according to rank).
- **Feldwebels (Sergeants Major):** Yellow silk braid with white celluloid stars.
- **Other NCOs and Gefreite (Corporals):** White celluloid stars.

c) Military Officials:

- Similar to equivalent officer ranks, but with **gold- and silver-embroidered rosettes instead of stars** (some exceptions retain stars).

For Naval Personnel:

- **Officers and officials** wear distinctions on their **tunics** like land forces.
- **Higher NCOs** display them on **cuffs of frock coats/jackets** and **shoulder boards of white jackets**; **flag officers** also wear them on **epaulettes**.
- **Lower NCOs and sailors** wear them on the **wide blue shirt collar**.

Additional Notes:

- **Generals' and staff officers' gold/silver braid** differs in design from that of civilian officials of equivalent rank (see color plates).
- **White-uniformed officers:** Silver stars (for subalterns) and white celluloid stars (for NCOs) have a **blue border**.
- **Cadets in Feldwebel rank:** The **yellow silk Feldwebel braid** is only **half-visible** over the **gold cadet braid**.

Insignia in Military (Landwehr) Educational Institutions

The distinction insignia for these institutions have already been mentioned in their respective uniform descriptions.

Non-Commissioned Personnel Not Assigned to a Pay Grade

Individuals such as **provosts (Profossen)**, **workshop foremen (Werkmeister)**, and **Landwehr district sergeants (Landwehr-Bezirksfeldwebel)** wear **Feldwebel (sergeant) distinctions**, but with **silver braid** (as previously described in the uniform regulations).

Bandmasters (Kapellmeister) – Army and Navy

- Wear a **gold-embroidered lyre** on each collar end.
- **Musicians** wear a **silver-plated lyra** as their insignia. For NCOs, this lyre is placed **before the rank stars**.

Secondary Distinction Insignia (By Rank Group)

Hat Braid (for Bicorne Hats)
- **Generals**: Gold braid, **8 cm wide**, with decorative patterning.
- **Staff Officers**: Gold braid, **6.6 cm wide**.

Czako/Czapka Braid (for Hungarian-style headgear)
- **Generals (in Hungarian uniform)**: Gold braid, **6.6 cm wide**.
- **Staff Officers**: Gold braid, **6.6 cm wide**, divided into **3 equal parts by 2 black longitudinal stripes**.
- **Captains (Hauptleute)**: Gold braid, **4.6 cm wide**, divided into **2 equal parts by 1 black stripe**.
- **Subaltern Officers**: Gold braid, **4 cm wide**.

For NCOs and Enlisted Men
- **Officer Deputies, Feldwebels, and Leaders**: Yellow silk/wool braid, **4.6 cm wide**, divided by **1 black stripe**.
- **Corporals (Korporals)**: Yellow braid, **4 cm wide**.
- **Gefreite (Lance Corporals)**: Yellow-and-black interwoven wool cord.

Navy Cap Braid
- Gold braid (**9 mm wide**) on the ribbed black moiré band of naval caps:
  - **Flag Officers**: 3 braids
  - **Staff Officers**: 2 braids
  - **Subaltern Officers**: 1 braid

ADDITIONAL INSIGNIA

Czako/Czapka/Hat Rosette
- **For Officers**:
  - Made of **gold bullion, 5 cm diameter**.
  - Center features the **imperial cipher "FJ" (Franz Joseph)** embroidered in gold on a black velvet field.
- **For NCOs and Soldiers**:
  - Pressed brass, **5 cm diameter**, with a black-lacquered center.
  - NCOs wearing bicorne hats use a **yellow silk rosette** (like officers).
- **For Military Officials**:
  - Same as officers, but with the **Imperial double eagle** in gold embroidery instead of the emperor's cipher.

Military Officials' Insignia

For military officials, the czako/hut rosette is similarly designed but only **3 cm in diameter**.

For NCOs and soldiers:
- Made of **yellow brass (3 cm diameter)** with the imperial cipher "FJ I" in openwork lettering
- Those wearing caps in officer style use a matching **yellow silk rosette**

For naval personnel:
- Yellow metal with black enamel, featuring the imperial cipher "FJ I"

Naval Cap Emblem

For naval officers, cadets, and officials:
- **Embroidered in gold and red silk**
- Features the imperial cipher "FJ I" over an **upright anchor**, surrounded by upward-curving laurel branches and topped with the **Imperial Crown**

For naval NCOs:
- **Imperial Crown** in stamped yellow metal
  - Senior NCOs: **3.5 cm wide**
  - Other NCOs: **3 cm wide**
- Below the crown, a rosette on black background with "FJ I" over an anchor

Hat Emblems
- Made of yellow and white metal (gilt/silvered for officers)
- Worn on the left side of the hat at the feather bush socket

Special designs:
- **Tyrolean units**: Yellow hunting horn with white Tyrolean eagle (Imperial eagle for Dalmatian units)
- **Feldjäger battalions & Landwehr infantry**: Yellow horn with white regimental numbers
- **Hungarian Gendarmerie**: Combined Austro-Hungarian coat of arms with crown and motto "For King and Fatherland"

Porte-Épée (Sword Knot)
- Consists of a strap and tassel, attached to the sword/dagger
- **Officers**: Gold and black silk with tassel buttons showing "FJ I" on one side and the **double eagle** on the reverse
- **NCOs**: Yellow and black silk/wool with checkered-pattern buttons
- **Infantry NCOs**: Smaller version
- **Naval officials**: Gold tassels with silver strap/button
- **Bandmasters**: Silver and red (officer-style)
- **Musicians**: In regimental facing colors with white (NCO-style)

Artillery Gun-Laying Cord
For artillery masters:
- **Scarlet wool** with large triple-ball tassels
- Worn diagonally from left shoulder to right hip

Skill Badges
A) Corded Badges (left breast):
- **Marksmanship**:
  - Infantry: Scarlet wool with ball tassels
  - Jägers/Landwehr: Grass-green
  - Sharpshooter: Gilt metal wire
- **Pioneer Helmsman**: Dark green
- **Railway/Telegraph**: As pioneer

B) Metal Cockades (right breast):
- **Distance Estimation**: Falcon design with laurel/oak wreath
- **Cavalry**: St. George image with wreaths
- **Machine Gun**: Three-headed dragon breathing fire under a crown
- **Artillery Aiming**: Crossed cannon barrels under crown
- **Driving (Artillery/Train)**: Harnessed horses with/without cannons
- **Sapper**: Crossed pickaxe/shovel
- **Telegrapher**: Lightning bolts under crown
- **Medical**: Red cross on white field

Service Accoutrements
Worn by combat troops during duty, parades, and field operations:
Field Sash:
- **Generals (German uniform)**: Gold/black silk
- **Staff/Line Officers**: Imperial yellow/black silk
- Worn:
  - Horizontally at waist (most officers)
  - Diagonally shoulder-to-hip (adjutants)

Waistbelts:
- **Generals (Hungarian uniform)**: 4.6 cm gold mesh with black cords
- **Honvéd officers**: 4.6 cm Isfahan wool with gold/black trim

Cartridge Pouches:
- **Mounted officers**: Gilt/silver fittings on red leather strap
- **NCOs**: Plain red leather

Gendarmerie Insignia
- Red leather crossbelt (officers: red morocco) with brass oval plate bearing the double eagle

Flags of the Imperial & Royal Army

Flags are carried as follows:

- **White Leibfahnen (Regimental Colors)**:: By every infantry and Kaiserjäger regiment.
  - White silk with Virgin Mary (obverse) and Imperial Eagle (reverse)
  - White Leibfahnen (Regimental Colors): By every infantry and Kaiserjäger regiment.
- **Yellow "Battle Honors" Flags**: By the 4th, 39th, 41st, and 57th Infantry Regiments (instead of the Leibfahne) in commemoration of glorious military deeds associated with them.

  The infantry regiments No. 81 to 102, established in 1883, were also issued yellow flags that had become available from the disbanded reserve commands at the time.
- All feature:
  - The flag panel (132 cm wide, 176 cm long) of the Leibfahne is made of white silk. Woven in gold, silver, and silk, it bears on one side the image of the Immaculate Mother of God and on the other the Imperial and Royal double-headed eagle with the coats of arms of all kingdoms and crown lands.
  - For the yellow flag, the panel is made of silk of that color and features the Imperial and Royal double-headed eagle on both sides, as with the Leibfahne.
  - The three free edges of both flag panels are adorned with a 12 cm-wide border of alternating red and silver, then black and gold flames in uniform sequence. The fourth edge is wrapped around the flagpole and secured with four rows of gilded nails, each row backed by a silk ribbon (red, white, black, yellow).
  - The flagpole (284 cm long) displays diagonal fields in the colors black, yellow, white, and red. At the top, it is decorated with a heart-shaped, gilded metal finial, engraved on both sides with the Imperial Crown and the monogram of His Majesty the Emperor.

During drills, marches, etc., the flag is carried in a protective case.

Flags of the Imperial and Royal Navy

These consist of red fabric with a white central stripe, upon which the Austrian coat of arms and the Imperial Crown are displayed in color,

Field Decorations

- Summer: Oak leaves
- Winter: Fir sprigs (laurel/boxwood for navy)
- Worn on headgear during parades and field service

They are worn on headgear during parades, in the field, and on other occasions specified in uniform regulations.

THE PLATES

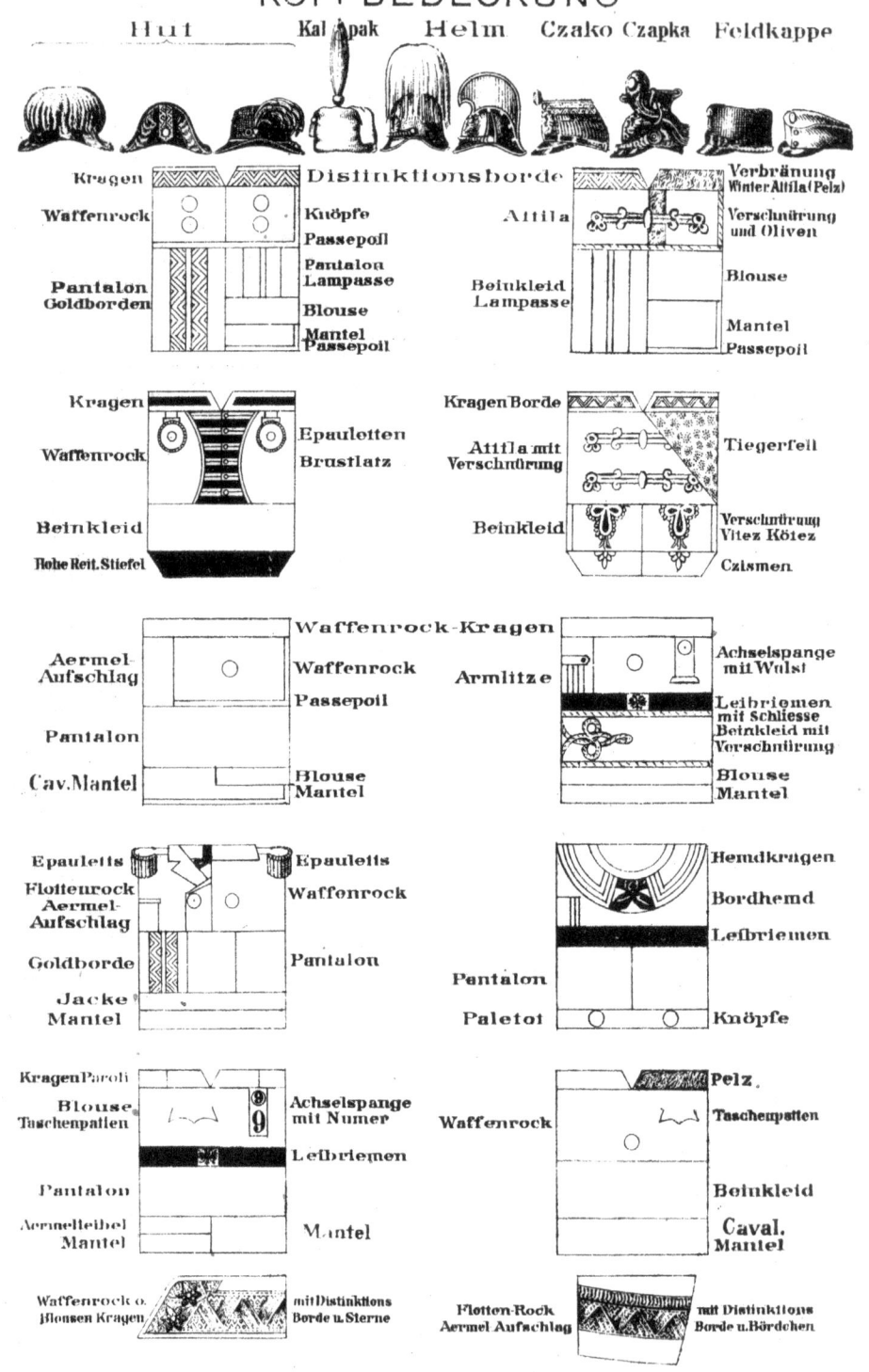

GENERALITÄT

General mit deutscher Uniform   General mit ungarisch. Uniform

Gala Uniform   *Dienst Uniform*   *Gala Uniform*   *Dienst Uniform*

CHEF D. GEN: STABES   GENERAL- & FLÜGEL-ADJUTANT

Gala Dienst   *Gala Dienst*   (S.M. des Kaisers: weisse Knöpfe)

GENERAL-ARTILLERIE-INSPEKTOR   GENERAL-GENIE-INSPEKTOR   GENERAL-AUDITOR   GENERAL-STABS-ARZT

Gala Dienst   *Gala Dienst*   *Gala Dienst*   *Gala Dienst*

MILITÄR BEAMTE MIT GENERALSRANG

GENERAL-INTENDANT   ARTILLERIE-GEN. INGENIEUR   GEN. BAU-INGENIEUR   MINIST.-RATH (RECH. CONTROLLE)

Gala Dienst   *Gala Dienst*   *Gala Dienst*   *Gala Dienst*

INFANTERIE
102 REGIMENTER

Offizier Nr. 1	Offiz.-Stellv	Mannschaft	Nr. 2	Nr. 3
Nr. 4	Nr. 5	Nr. 6	Nr. 7	Nr. 8
Nr. 9	Nr. 10	Nr. 11	Nr. 12	Nr. 13
Nr. 14	Nr. 15	Nr. 16	Nr. 17	Nr. 18

4

INFANTERIE

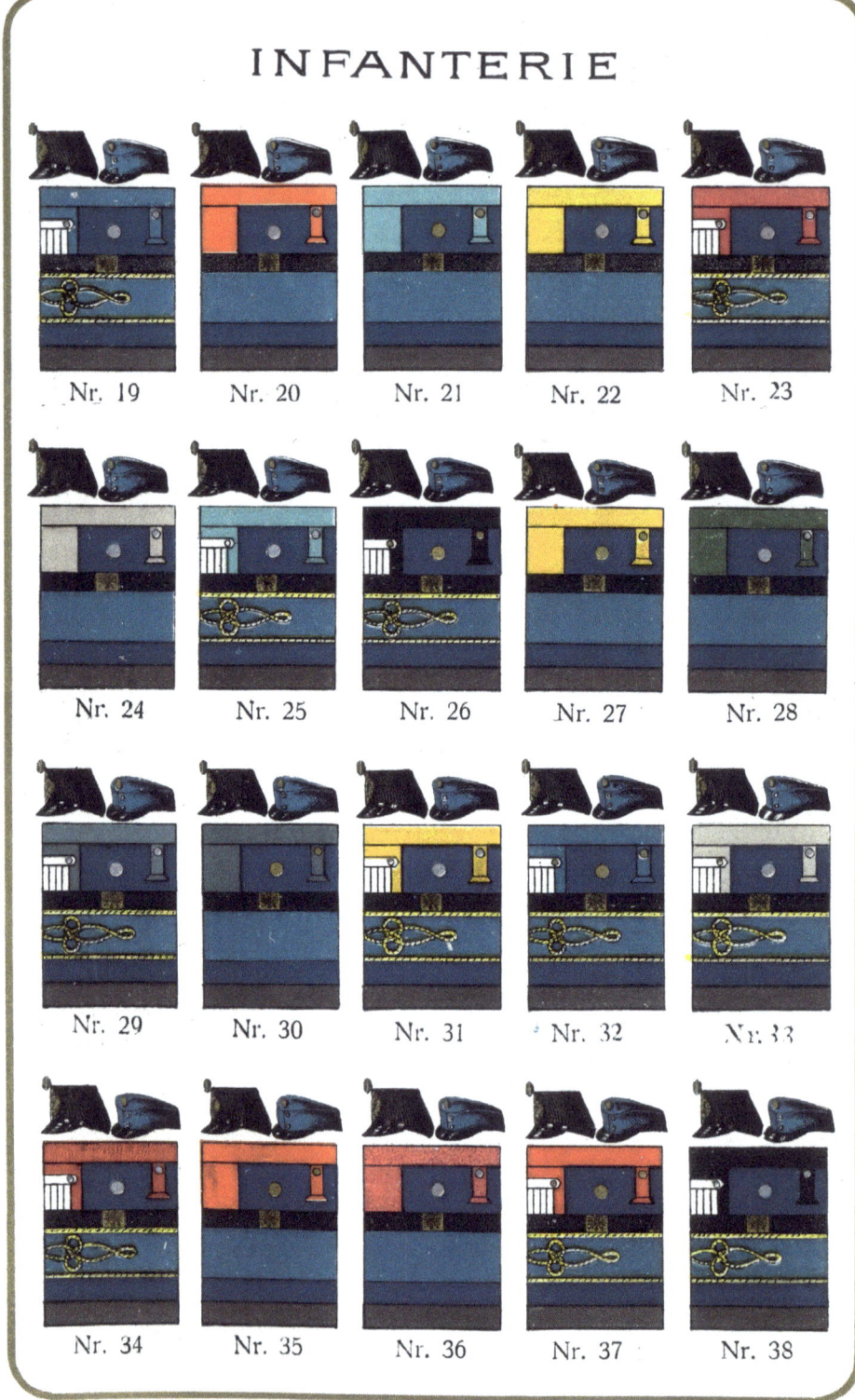

INFANTERIE

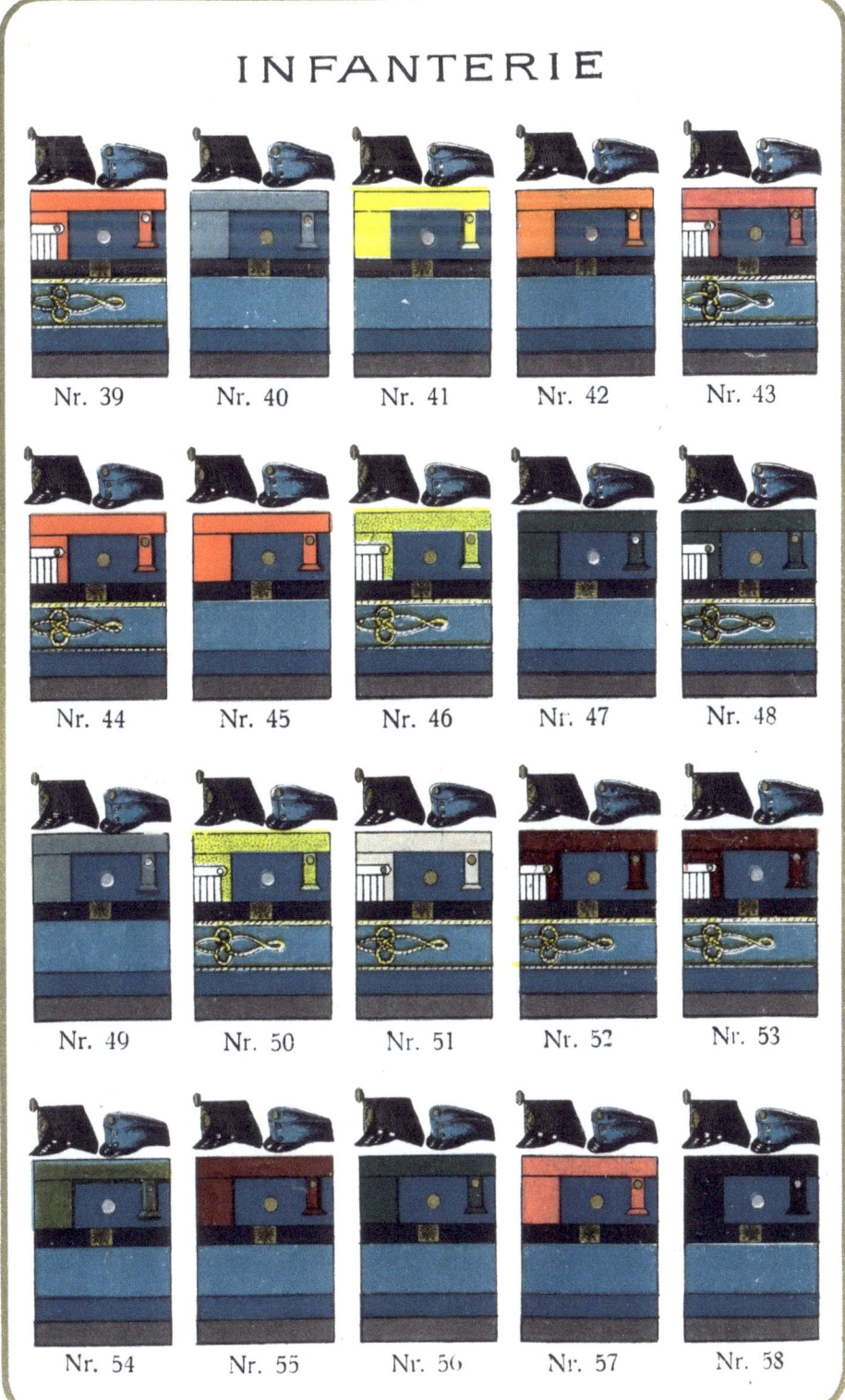

INFANTERIE

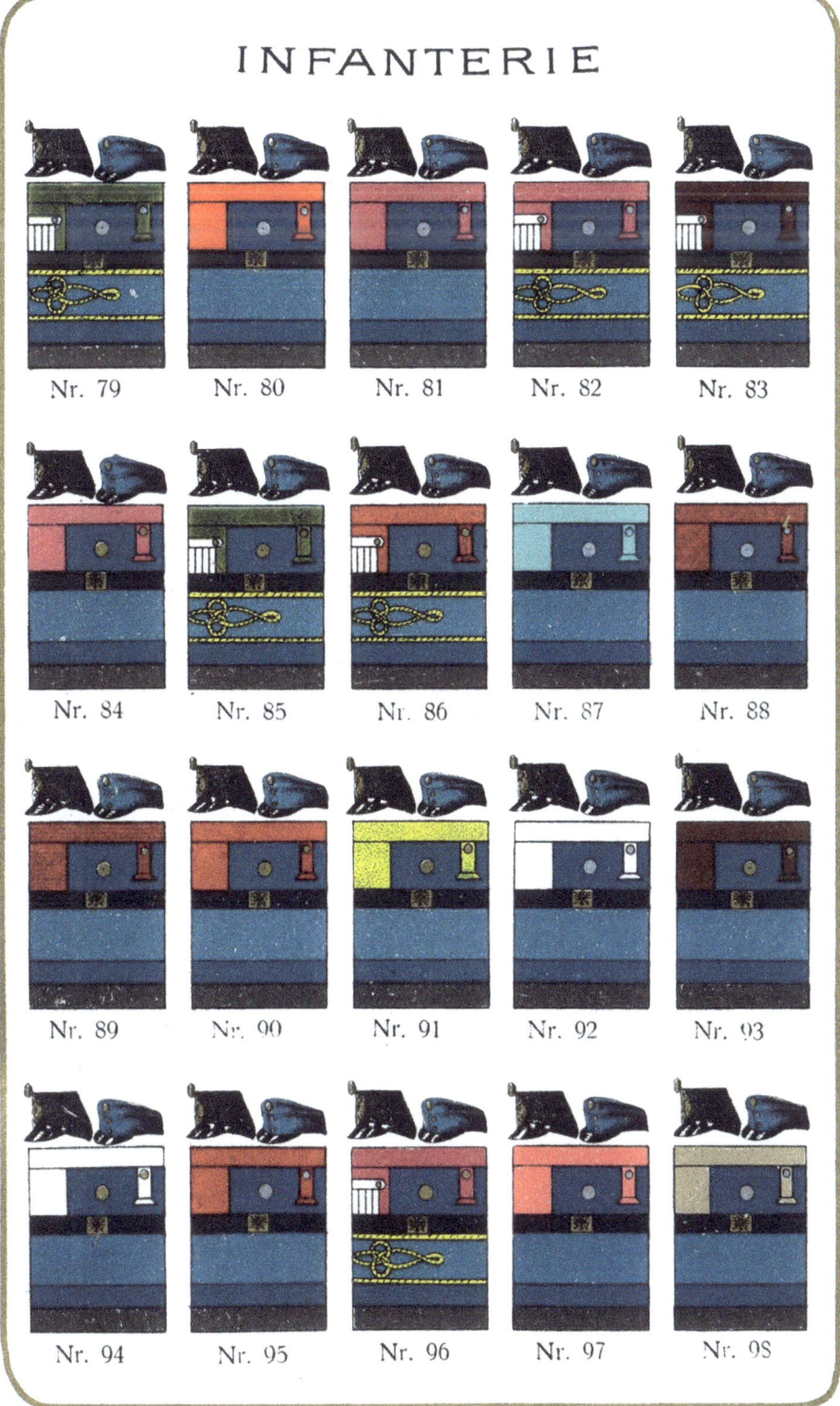

8

INFANTERIE

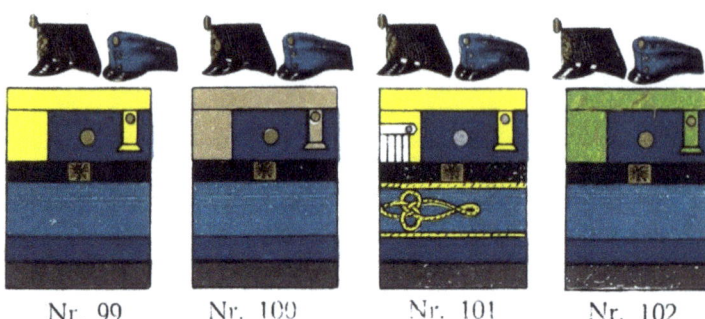

Nr. 99   Nr. 100   Nr. 101   Nr. 102

EGALISIRUNGS-FARBEN-SCHEMA DER INFANTERIE

		DEUTSCH		UNGAR				DEUTSCH		UNGAR	
		g	w	g	w			g	w	g	w
		KNÖPFE						KNÖPFE			
Dunkel-		1	18	52	53	Orange-		59	42	64	63
Bordeaux-		89	88			Kaiser-	gelb	27	22	2	31
Krapp-		15	74	44	34	Schwefel-		99	41	16	101
Amarant-		90	95	86		Stahl-		56	47	48	60
Kirsch-		73	77	43	23	Gras-		8	28	61	62
Carmoisin-	roth	84	81	96	82	Apfel-	grün	9	54	85	79
Scharlach-		45	80	37	39	Meer-Gras-		102			
Krebs-		35	20	71	67	Meer-		21	87	70	25
blass-		57	36	65	66	Papagei-		91	10	46	50
Rosen-		13	97	5	6	Himmel-		4	3	32	19
Dunkel-		93	7	12	83	licht-	blau	40	75	72	29
Roth-	braun	55	17	68	78	licht-	drapp	100	98		
weiss		94	92			Hecht-		30	49	76	69
schwarz		14	58	26	38	Asch-	grau	11	24	51	33

JÄGER-TRUPPE

TIROLER KAIS. JÄG. REGMT. 1-4   FELD-JÄGER-BATAILLONE (26)

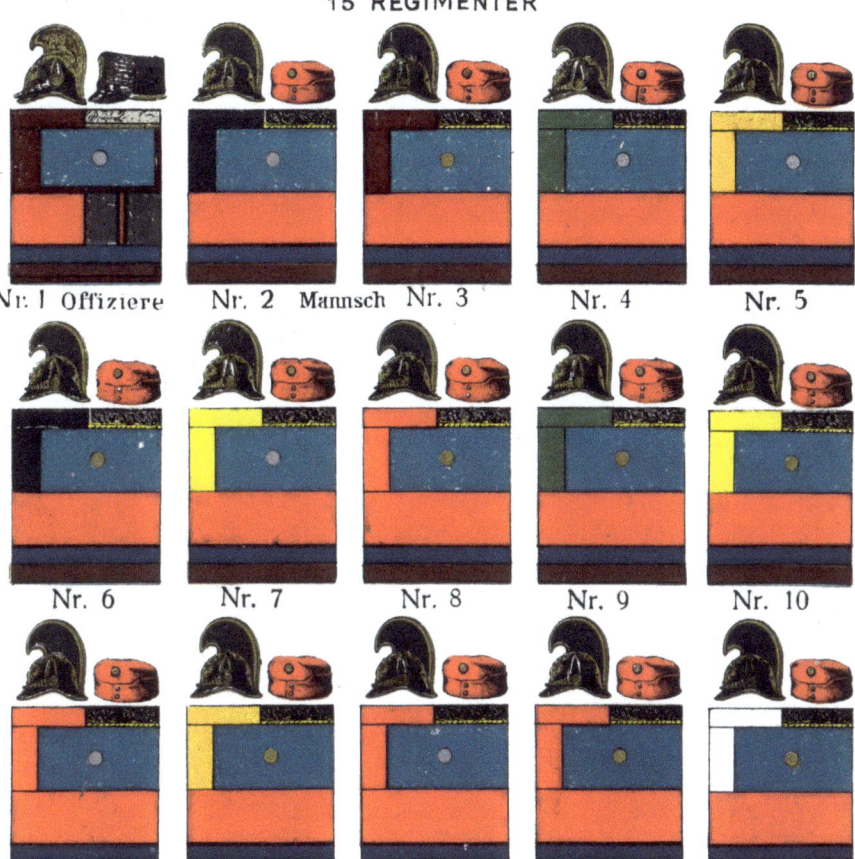

Offiziere — Mannschaft — Offiziere — Mannschaft

KAVALLERIE.
DRAGONER.
15 REGIMENTER

Nr. 1 Offiziere — Nr. 2 Mannsch — Nr. 3 — Nr. 4 — Nr. 5
Nr. 6 — Nr. 7 — Nr. 8 — Nr. 9 — Nr. 10
Nr. 11 — Nr. 12 — Nr. 13 — Nr. 14 — Nr. 15

HUSZAREN
16 REGIMENTER

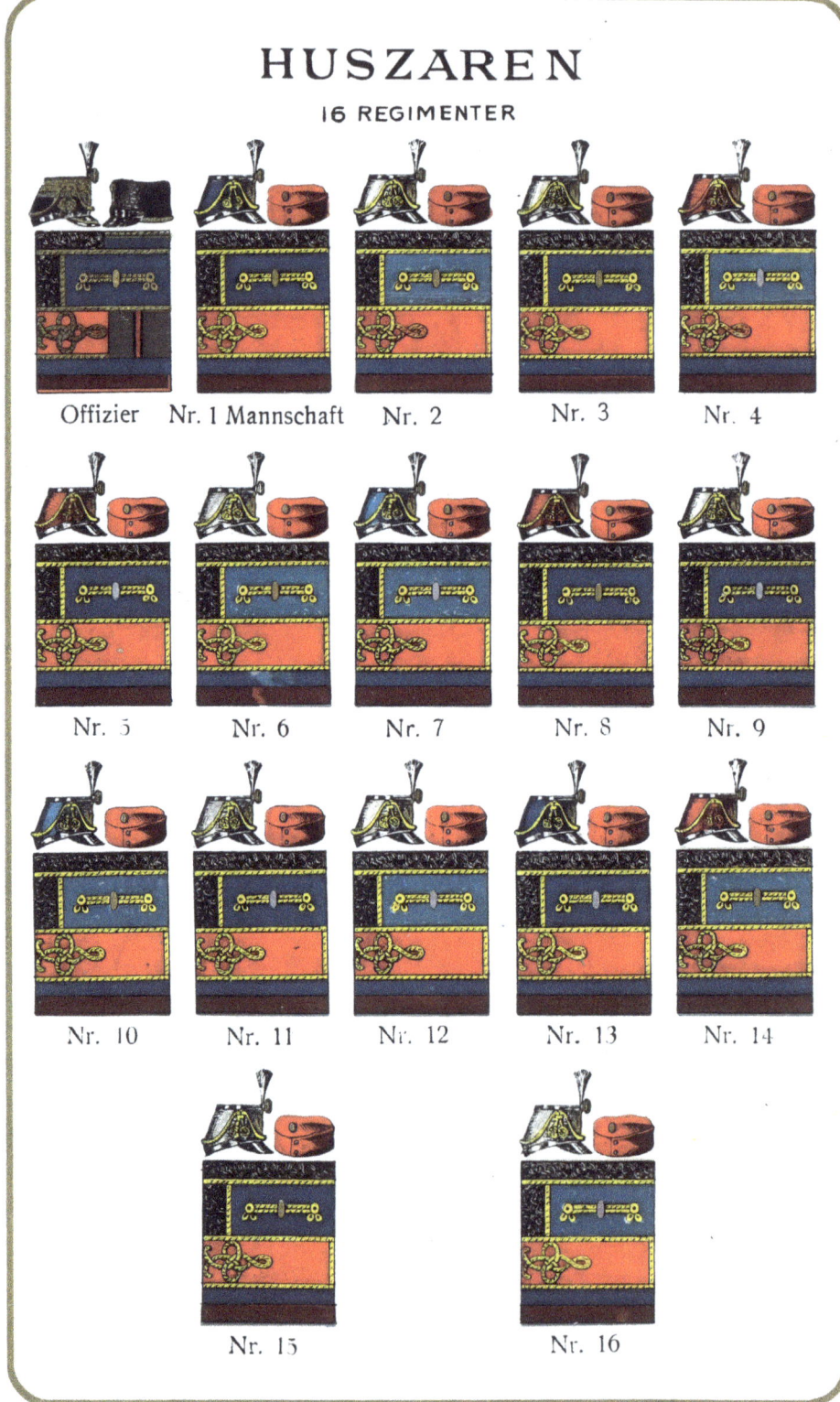

Offizier, Nr. 1 Mannschaft, Nr. 2, Nr. 3, Nr. 4, Nr. 5, Nr. 6, Nr. 7, Nr. 8, Nr. 9, Nr. 10, Nr. 11, Nr. 12, Nr. 13, Nr. 14, Nr. 15, Nr. 16

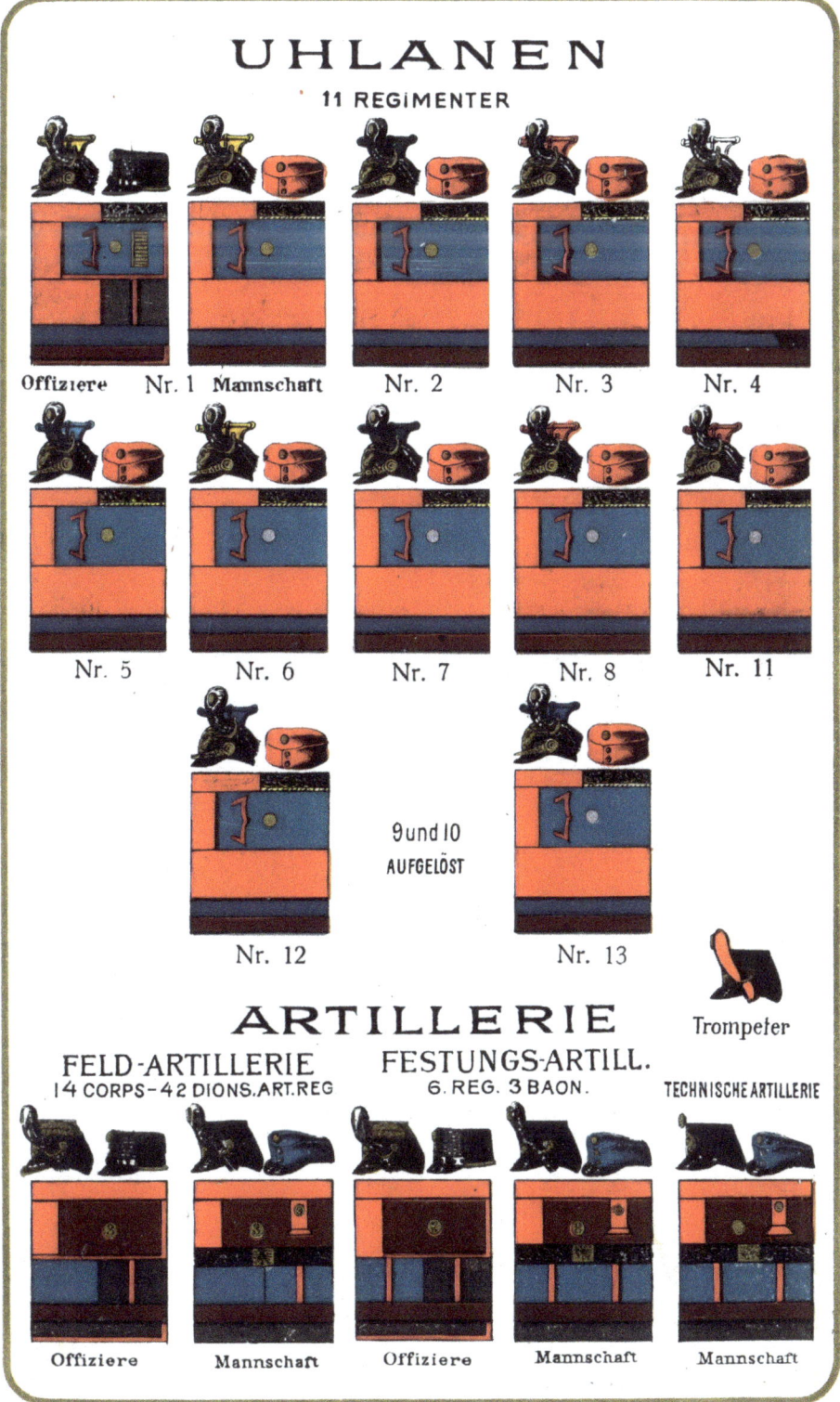

PIONNIER-TRUPPE
15. BAONE

Offiziere

Mannschaft

EISENBAHN-REGM.

Offiziere

Mannschaft

SANITÄTS-TRUPPE

Offiziere

Mannschaft

TRAIN-TRUPPE

Offiziere   Mannsch.(GebirgsT.)

MONTUR-BRANCHE

Offiziere

Mannschaft

VERPFLEGS-BRANCHE

Mannschaft

MIL.GEOGR:INSTITUT

Mannschaft

OFFIZIER D.ARMEE-STANDES

INVALIDEN-CORPS

Offiziere

Mannsch.

MILT. KAPELLMEISTER

(Regmts.Egalisg.)

MILITÄR BILDUNGS-ANSTALTEN
A. ZÖGLINGE
KADETENSCHULEN FÜR:

INFANTERIE	KAVALLERIE	ARTILLERIE	PIONNIERE

OFFIZ. WAISEN INSTITUT	MILIT. UNTER REAL-SCHULE	MILIT. OBER REAL-SCHULE	MIL. AKADEMIEN (AKADEMIKER)

B. LEHR- & AUFSICHTS-PERSONALE

LEHR- u. INSPEK. U. OFFZ.	REIT-LEHRER-GEHILFEN	

in sämtl. Anstalten u. Fecht-u.Turn-Lehr-Curs	Reit Lehrer Institut u. Milit. Akademie	Techn. Milt. Akademie

C. MANNSCHAFT

Spielleute	Hausdiener	THIERARZNEI-INSTITUT

in sämtl. Milit Bildungs-Anstalten		Mannschaft

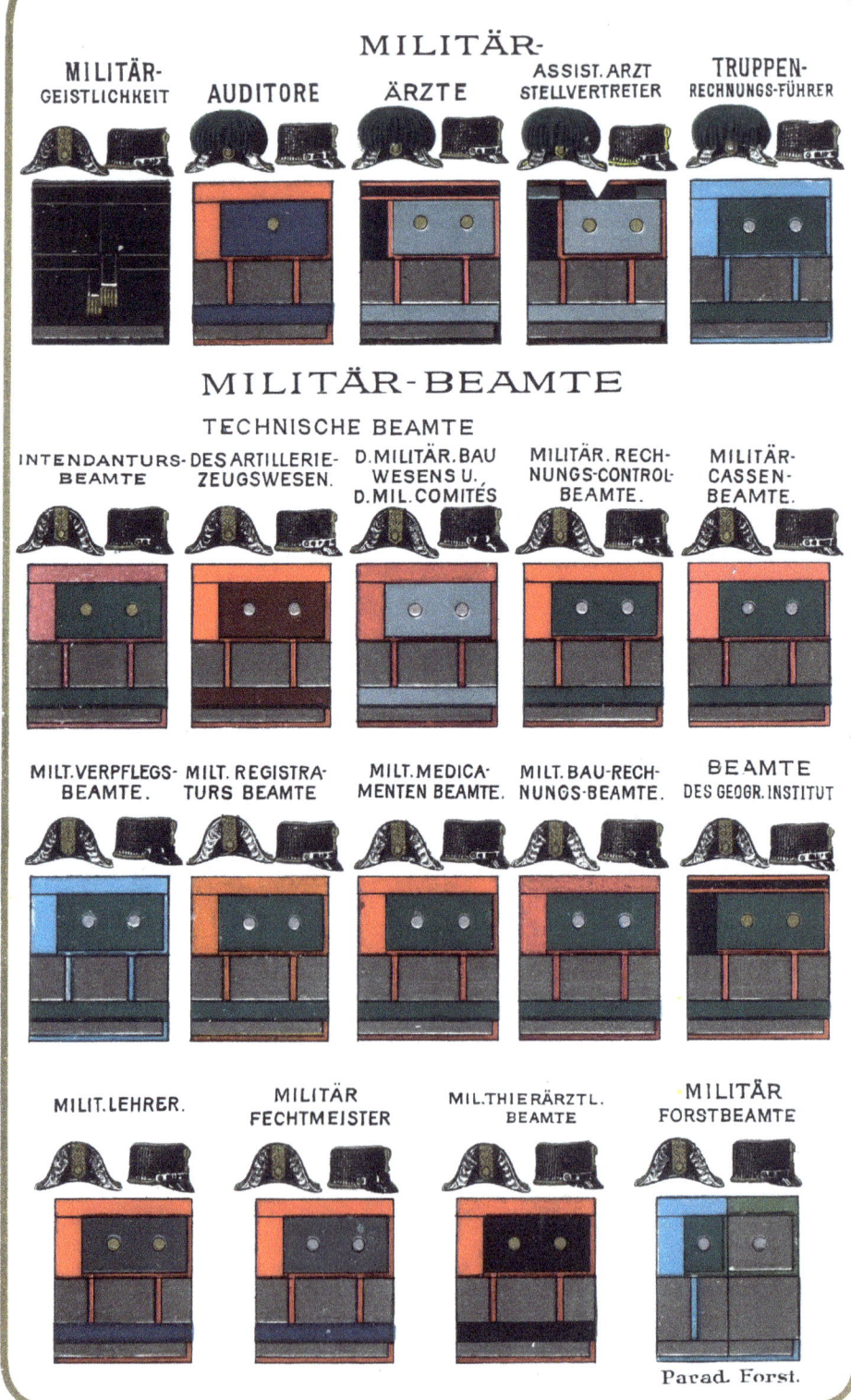

TECHNISCHES HILFSPERSONAL

PROFOSS — **WERKMEISTER / OB. WAFFENMEISTER** — **BAUWERKMEISTER**

DEM HEERES-VERBANDE NICHT EINVERLEIBTE MILITÄR-ABTHEILUNGEN

K.K. LANDES-GENDARMERIE — **UNG. GENDARMERIE**

Offz. 1–14 — Mannsch. — RECHNUNGS-FÜHRER — Offz. — Mannsch.

MILT. POLIZEI-WACHCORPS — **WACHCORPS F. CIVILGERICHTE**

Mannschaft — Mannschaft

GESTÜTS-BRANCHE

K.K. HENGSTEN-DEPOTS — **UNG. PFERDEZUCHTANSTALTEN**

Offiz. — Mannsch. — Offiz. — Mannsch.

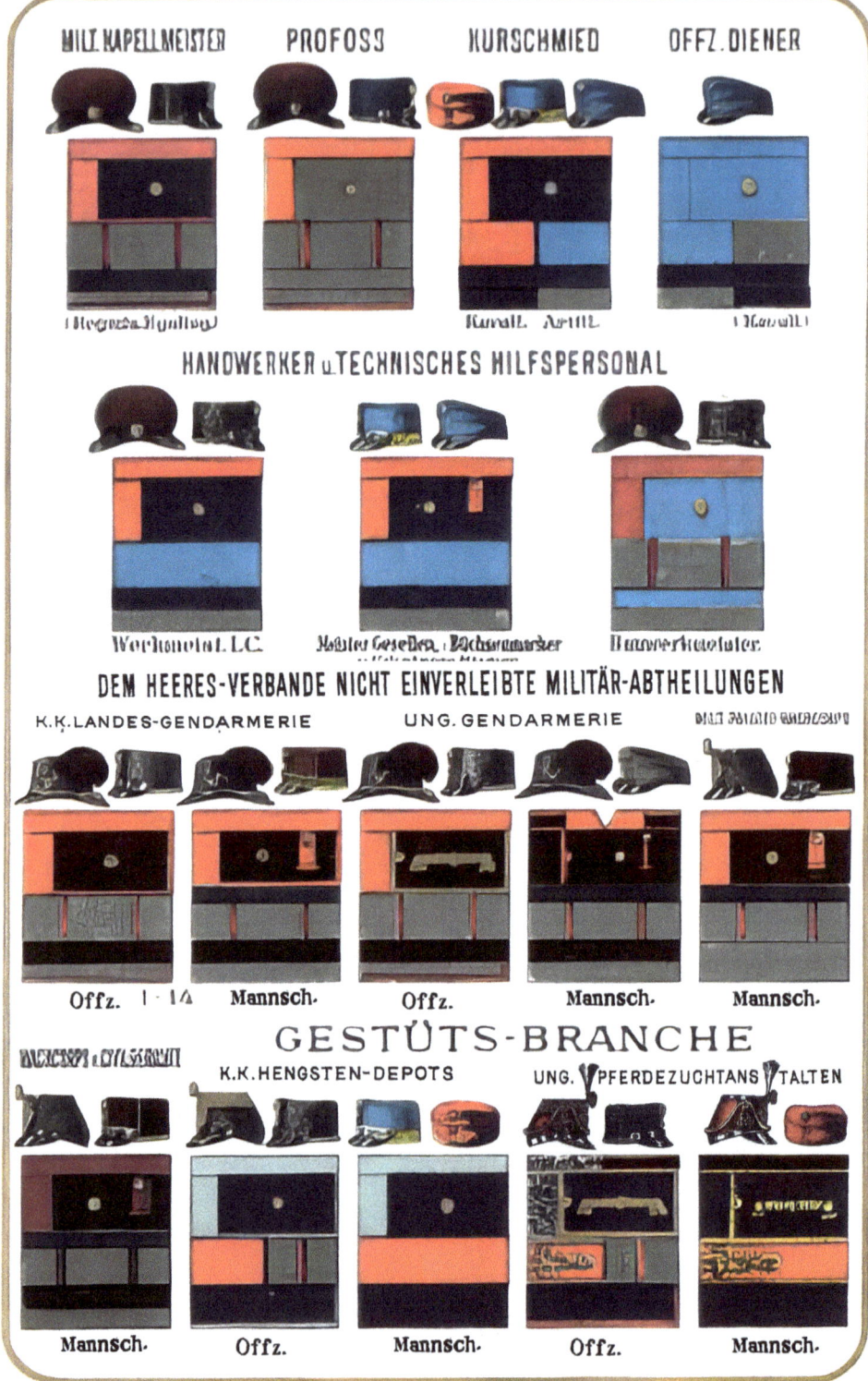

16

K.K. KRIEGS-MARINE

SEE-OFFIZIERE | SEE-KADETEN

- Gala Parad
- Gross. Dienst Unifo.
- Gew. Uniform
- Grosse Dienst Unif.

HÖHERE UNT. OFFIZ. | UNT. OFFZ. & MATROSEN | MUSIK-MANNSCHAFT

MAR. AKADEMIE | MAR. ARZT | MAR. TECHN. BEAMTE | MAR. KOMISSARIATS-BEAMTE

Zöglinge

MAR. BEAMTE F. HYDR. u. LEHRFACH | MAR. KAPELLMEISTER | OFFZ. DIENER

K.K. LANDWEHR
FUSSTRUPPEN

| LANDW. INFANTERIE | LANDESSCHÜTZEN |
| 36 REGIMENTER | 2 REGIMENTER |

Offz.   Offz.Stellv.   Mannschaft   Offz.   Mannsch.

BERITTENE LANDW.-TRUPPEN
LANDW. UHLANEN
6. REG.

 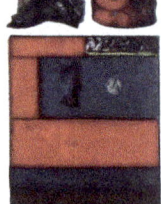

Offz.   Mannsch.

| BERITTENE TIROLER LANDESSCHÜTZEN | BERITTENE DALMAT. LANDESSCHÜTZEN |

Offz.   Mannsch.   Offz.   Mannsch.

| LANDW. | LW KADETENSCHULE | LANDW. AUSRÜSTUNGS |
| BEZIRKS-FELDWEBEL | ZÖGLINGE | HAUPT-DEPOT WIEN |

 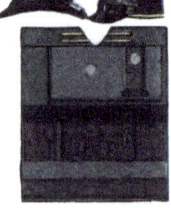  

WERKMEISTER   Mannsch.

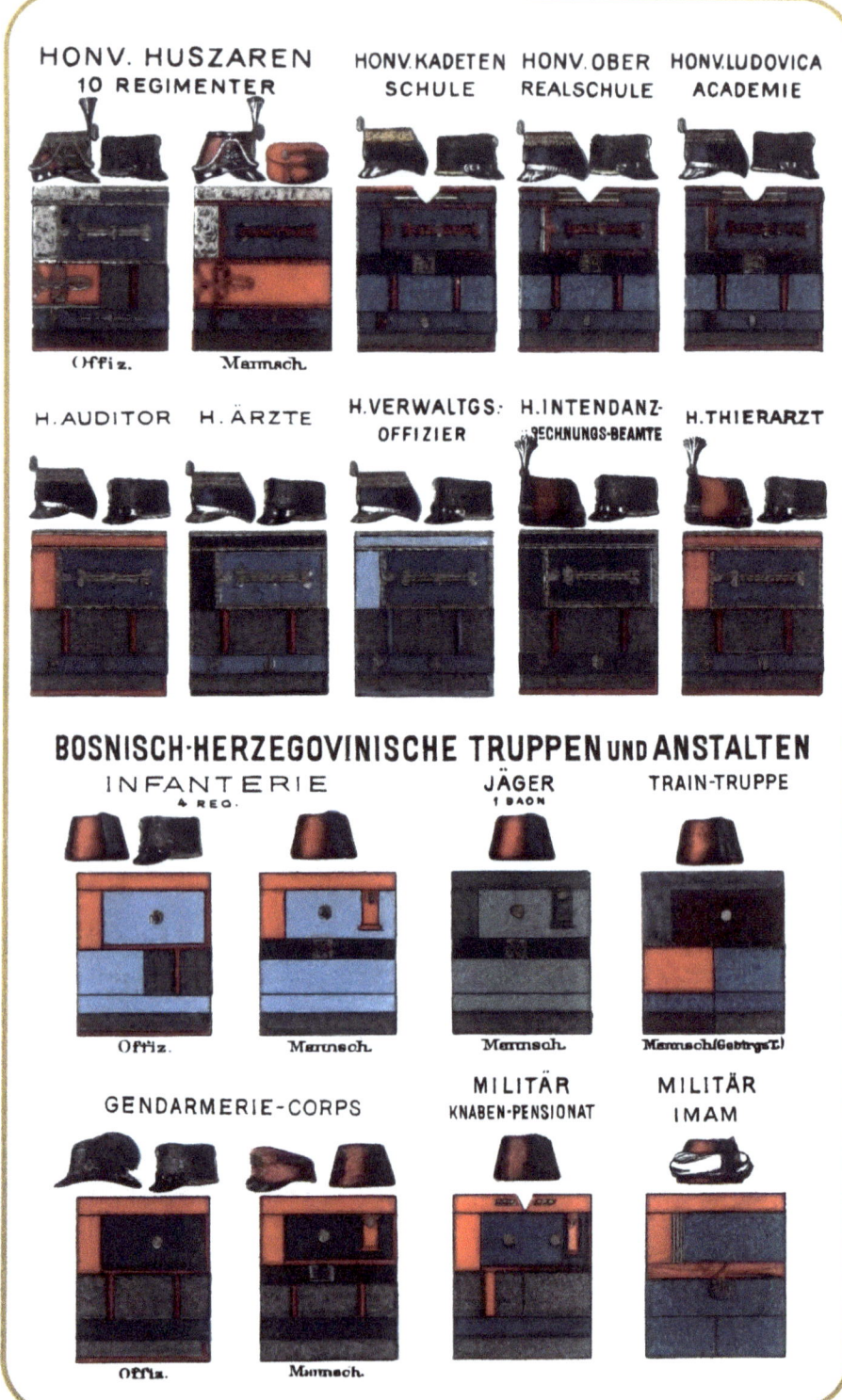

LANDSTURM

ÖSTERREICH		UNGARN		DELEGIRTE VOM ROTHEN KREUZ
Offz.	Mannschaft	Offiz.	Mannsch.	

ABZEICHEN
FÜR VERSCHIEDENE DIENSTKATEGORIEN
ARMBINDEN ALS ABZEICHEN FÜR:

| Österreich | Landsturm in Tirol | Ungarn | Sanitäts Personal | Ober Stabs Wagenmeister | Stabs Wagenmeister | Wagenmeister | Stabstruppen u Civil |

wenn (sonst eigene Kleidung)

ABZEICHEN AM ÄRMEL FÜR

| EINJÄHRIG FREIWILLIGE | AKADEMIKER LETZTER JG. | PHARMACEUTEN U VETERINÄRE EINJ. FREIW. | WAFFENMEIST. KURSCHMIEDE ESCAD. RIEMER | FREIW. LÄNGER DIENENDE UNTEROFFIZIERE | OFFIZIERSDIEN UND PFERDE WÄRTER. |

AUF BEIDEN ÄRMELN — AM LINKEN ÄRMEL — AM RECHTEN ÄRMEL

ABZ. AM ÄRMEL F. D. SPECIALITÄTEN DER MARINE MANNSCHAFT

| Deck-Dienst | Steuer-Dienst | Maschinen-Dst. | Waffen Dienst | Artillerie Dienst | Sanitäts-Dienst |
| vom Quartiermeister aufwärts m. Krone | | | | Instructor Vormeister | Krankenwärter |

vom Gast abwärts ohne Krone — Kanonier — Quartiers Abzeichen

DISTINCTIONS-ABZEICHEN
GENERALITÄT (FLAGGEN-OFFIZIERE)

Feldmarschall 1	Feldzeugmeist.(Gen&.C*v*) 3	Feldmarsch.Lieut. 4	Generalmajor 5

Auf den Epauletten u. Aermelaufschlag des Flottenrockes der Marine.

Admiral	Vice Admiral	Contre Admiral

STABS-OFFIZIERE

Oberst des Gen. Stab Ober Stabs-Arzt 1.Cl 6	Oberst des Infr. Rg. N°15 Oberst-Auditor 6	Oberstlieut. I.R.N°3 " Auditor Oberstabsarzt 2.C. 7	Major I.R.N°28 " Auditor Stabs-Arzt 8

Oberster Mar. Arzt	Linien- Schiffs-Capitän	Fregatten-Capitän Mar. Ober Stabs-Arzt	Corvetten-Capitän Mar. Stabs-Arzt

OBER-OFFIZIERE

Hauptmann des Gen. Stab. Regmts. Arzt 9	(Rittmeister) des Infr. Reg. N°40 Haupm. Auditor 9	Oberlieut. I.R.N°92 " Auditor Ober-Arzt 10	Lieutenant. Infr. Reg. N°58 Assistenz-Arzt 11

Lin. Schiff's Arzt u. Fregatten-Arzt	Lin. Schiffs Lieut.	Linen Schiff Fähnrich Corvetten-Arzt	Assistenz-Arzt

UNTEROFFIZIERE U. SOLDATEN

Cadet Offiziers Stellvertreter	Cadet-Feldwebel. C.Obergr.,C.Wachtmstr. Cadet-Feuerwerker	Feldwebel Obergr., Wachtmstr. Feuerwrkr., Waffenmeist. 1.C. etc.	Regiments Tambour Musik-Feldwebel

HÖHERE MAR. UNTEROFFIZIERE (FELDWEBELSRANG)

See-Cadet	Ober-Bootsmann, Ober-Steuermann, Ober-Maschinenwärter	Bootsmann, Steuermann, Maschinenwärten Waffenmeister	Unter Bootsmann, U. Steuerm., U. Maschnwrt. U. Waffenmstr., Corps-Hornist.

Zugs-(Stabs-)Führer Waffenmeister 2.Cl. Curschmied etc.	Corporal Unergra. Geschütz Vormstr. Waffenmeister 3.Cls. etc.	Gefreiten Patrullführer, Vormeisten Geselle 1.Cls.	Infanterist Jäger, Dragoner, Husar, Uhlan. Ober (Unt) K. monder etc.

Bootmanns-Maat Steuermanns, Maschinen Waffen; Sanitäts-Maat	Mars, Steuer-Gast. Maschinen Waffen Sanitäts Gast und Quartiermeister	Matrose 1.Cls. Steuer Matrose, Heizer 1.C., Krankenwärter 1.Cl.	Matrose 2-4 C. Heizer 2.C. Krankenwärter 2. u. 3. C.

Hemd Kragen

* Die Ziffern bedeuten die Diäten-Classe

DISTINCTIONS-ABZEICHEN
MILITÄR-BEAMTE

General Intendant etc. (Sektions Chef 2 Sterne)	Ober-Intendant etc. 1.Cls.	2.Cls.	Intendant etc.	Unt.Intendant etc.
5	6	7	8	9

Ministerial-Rath	Ober-Rechnungsrath, Cassen-Direktor u. Oberpflegsverwalter 1.Cls. Registrat Direktor etc.	2.Cls. Registr.Unt.Direkt., Medikament-Ober Verwalter etc.	Rechnungs-Rath, Zahlmeister, Verpflegs-Verwalt., Registrator, Medikament Verwalt., Bau-Rechngs-Rath etc.
5	6	7	8

| Mar. General-Commissär | Oberster Ingenieur, Ober-Commissär 1.Cl. Direktor etc. | Ober-Ingenieur 1.Cl. " Comissär 2.Cl., Abtheilungs-Vorstand etc. | Ober-Ingenieur 2.3.Cl. Ober-Maschinist, Comissär.Abtlgs.Vorstand. |

Rechnungs, Cassen, Verpflegs, Registraturs, Medikamenten, Bau-Rechnungs-etc.

-Offizial 1.u.2.Cl. Ober-Thierarzt 1.2.Cl.	-Offizial 3.Cl. Thierarzt	Accessist, Unt.Thierarzt etc.	Militär-Kapellmeister
9	10	11	

| Ingenieur-Maschinist u. Comissariats-Adjunkt 1.u.2.Cls. | 3.Cls. Oberwerkführer etc. | Werkführer etc. | Marine Kapellmeister |

ZÖGLINGE D. MILIT. BILDUNGS-ANSTALTEN

EINFACHE	DOPPELTE AUSZEICHNUNG		UNTEROFFICIERS-
Cadeten u.	Realschulen	Pion. Cadet. Schule	Akademien

HUT-BORDE FÜR: Generale, Stabsoffiziere **CZAKO-BORDE FÜR:** Hauptleute, Oberlieut. u. Lieutent., Feldwebel u. Führer **SCHNUR f.** Corporale, Gefreite

BORDKAPPEN-BÖRDCHEN FÜR: Flaggen- Stabs- Ober Offiz.

NACHTRAG.
TRUPPEN IN HECHTGRAUER FELDMONTUR
INFANTERIE.

| Offizier | Fähnrich N⁰ 1 | Mannschaft | Nr 2. | Nr. 3. u.s.w. |

JÄGER-TRUPPE   **PIONIER-TRUPPE**   **EISB:u.TEL.RGT.**

| Offiziere | Mannschaft | Offiziere | Mannschaft | Mannschaft |

SANITÄTS-TRUPPE.   **VERPFL-BRANCHE**   **BOSN. HERZOG. INFANTERIE**

| Offiziere | Mannschaft | Mannschaft | Offiziere | Mannschaft |

BOS.H.JÄGER   **LANDWEHR-INFANTERIE**   **LANDES-SCHÜTZEN**

    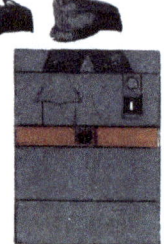

| Mannschaft | Offiziere | Mannschaft | Offiziere | Mannschaft |

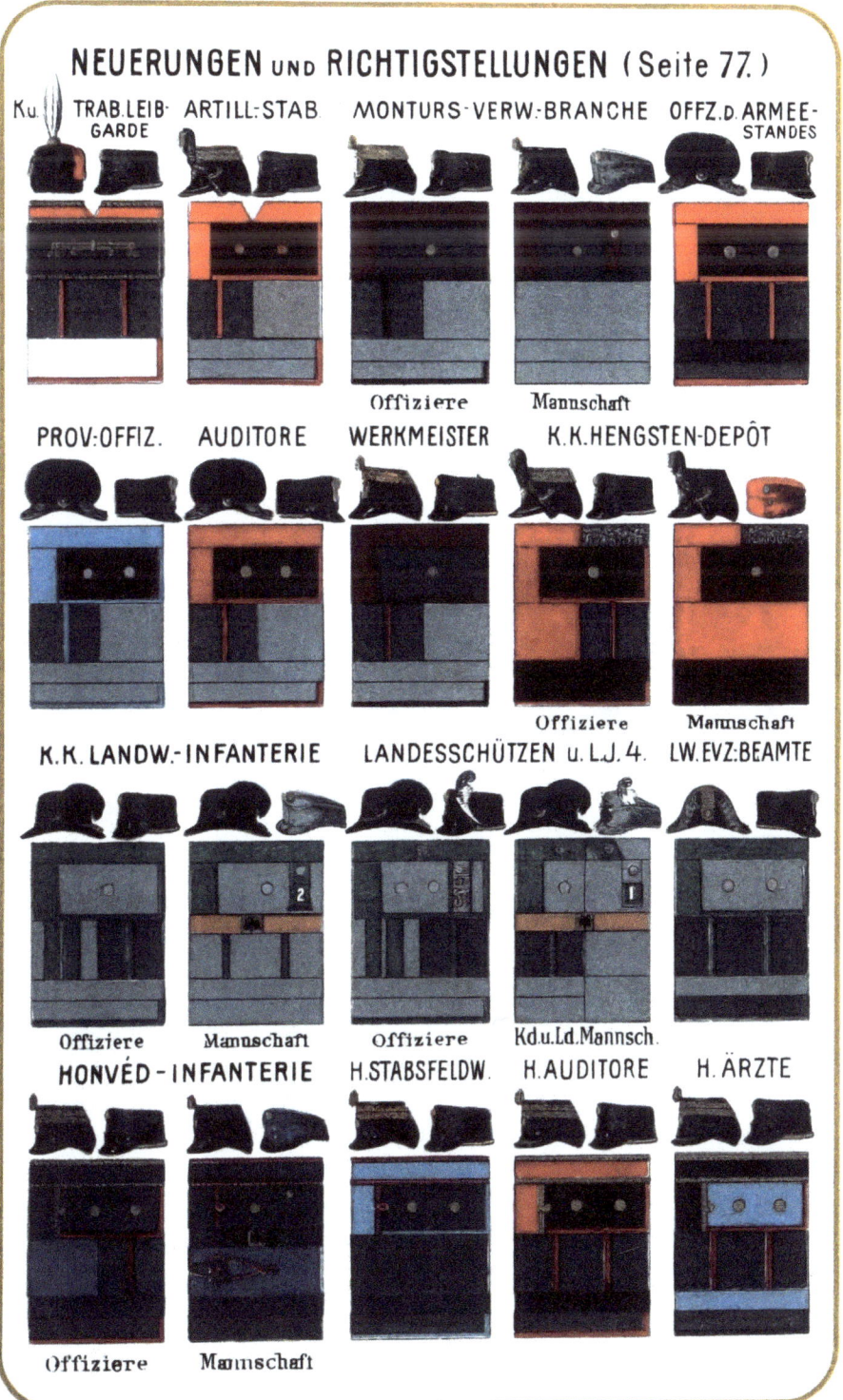

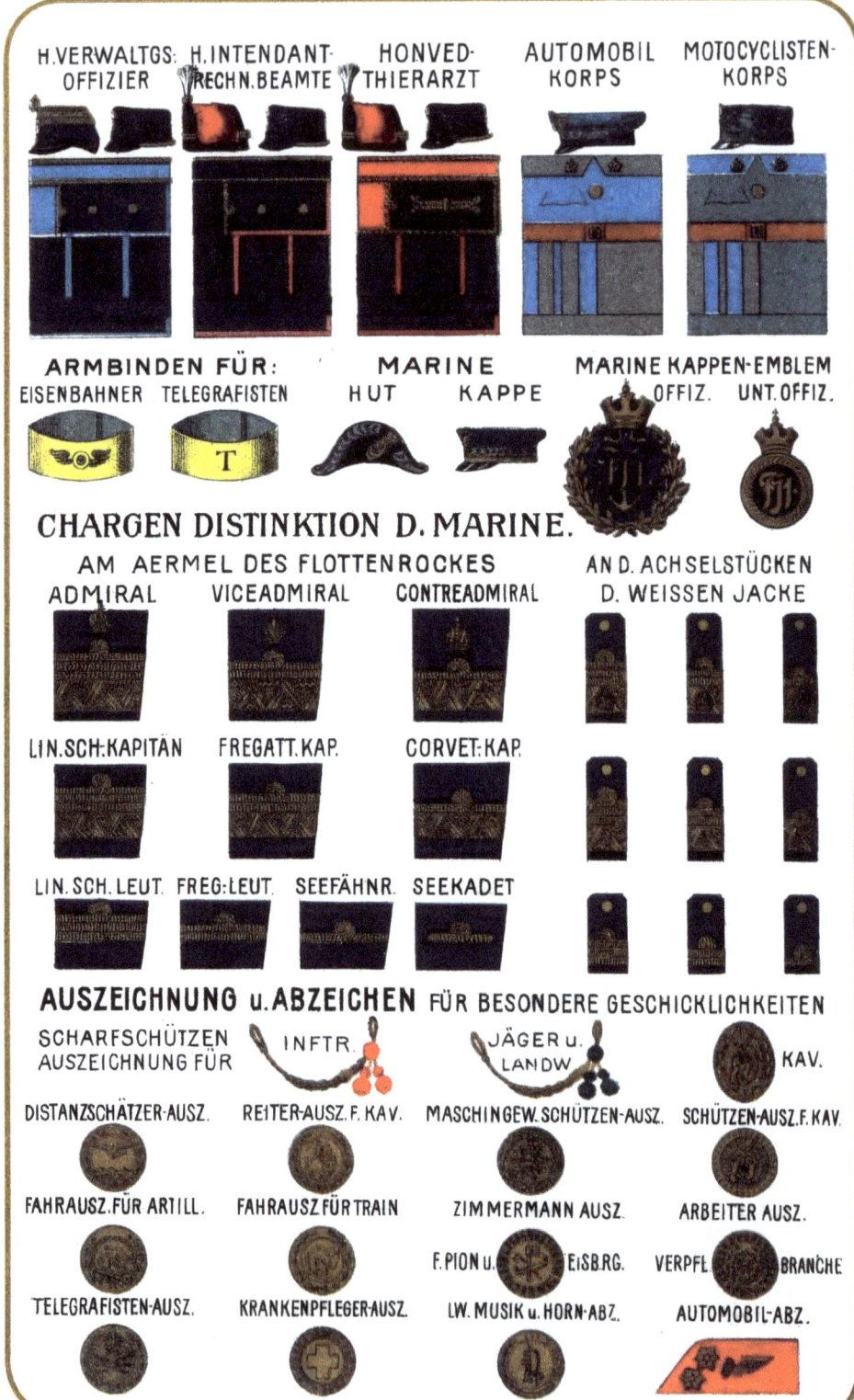

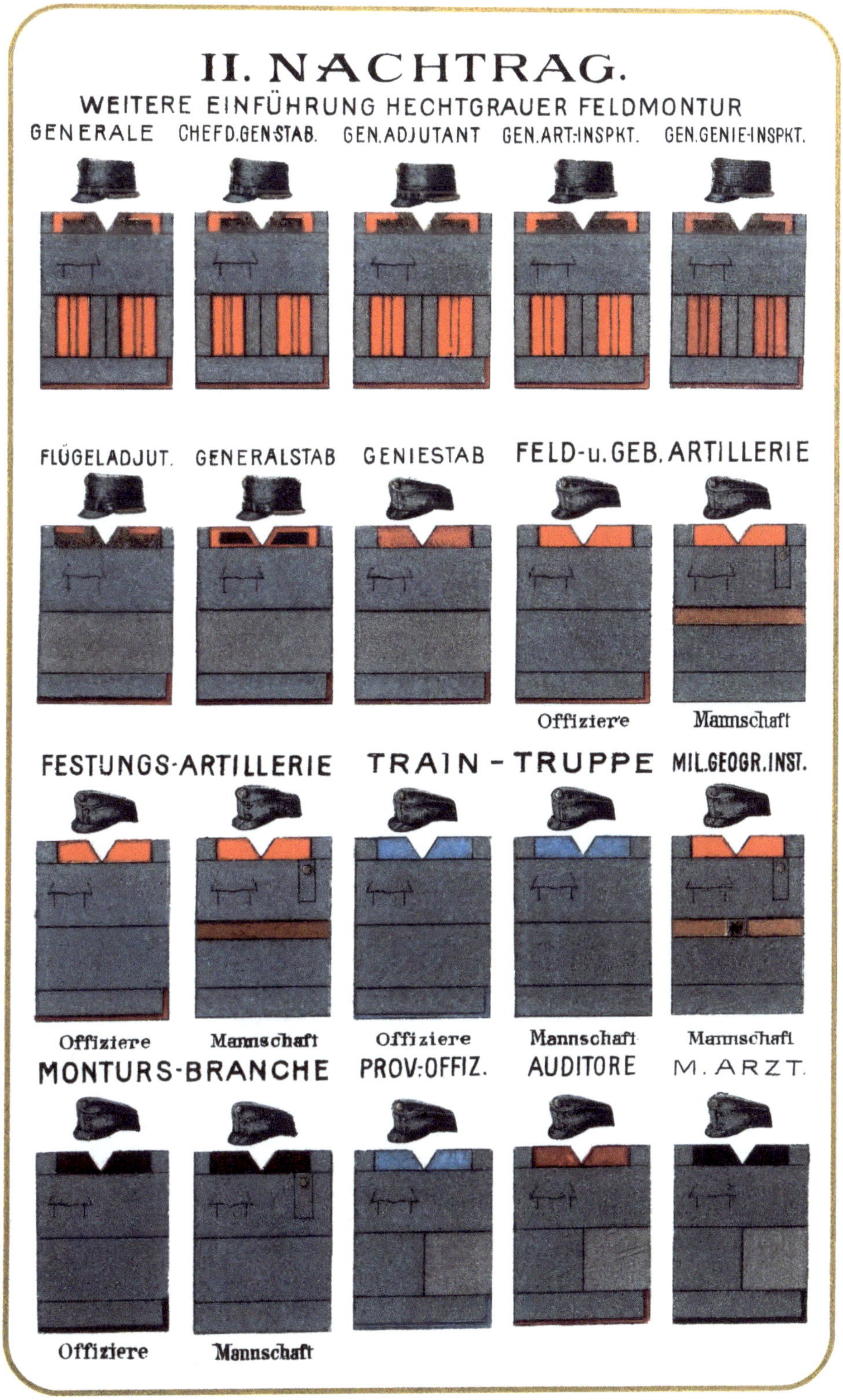

II. NACHTRAG.
WEITERE EINFÜHRUNG HECHTGRAUER FELDMONTUR

GENERALE	CHEF D. GEN. STAB.	GEN. ADJUTANT	GEN. ART. INSPKT.	GEN. GENIE-INSPKT.

FLÜGELADJUT.   **GENERALSTAB**   **GENIESTAB**   **FELD- u. GEB. ARTILLERIE**

Offiziere   Mannschaft

FESTUNGS-ARTILLERIE   **TRAIN-TRUPPE**   **MIL. GEOGR. INST.**

Offiziere   Mannschaft   Offiziere   Mannschaft   Mannschaft

MONTURS-BRANCHE   **PROV. OFFIZ.**   **AUDITORE**   **M. ARZT.**

Offiziere   Mannschaft

ORDEN u. EHRENZEICHEN

KRIEGS-MEDAILLE	ERINNERUNGS-MEDAILLE A.D. FELDZUG 1864 o. DÄN	DENKMÜNZE A.D. TIROLER LANDESVERTHEIDIGUNG	
		1848	1860

OFFIZIERS DIENSTZEICHEN
III. CLASSE   II. CLASSE

MANNSCHAFTS DIENSTZEICHEN
II. CLASSE   I. CLASSE

SOUVERAINE ORDEN
DEUTSCHER ORDEN

HALS-KREUZ   BRUST-KREUZ DER PROFESS RITTER   MARIANER-KREUZ

JOHAN. RITTER o. MALTÄSER ORDEN

▲ Portrait of Kaiser Franz Joseph in a piant of 1910 around. BundesmobilienverwaltungWien

APPENDIX

THE PLATES

OF THE WORK OF J.V.KULAS, FREDERICH FRANCESCHINI, MORITZ RUHL

"DIE OESTERREICH.-UNGARISCHE ARMEE" (VOR 1881/82) VERLAG MORITZ RUHL

Illustrations of the German and Hungarian troops, the Landwehr and Navy as well as the Bosnian-Hercegovinian and Tyrolean border troops - edited by Verlag Moritz Ruhl, Leipzig around 1881.

Characteristics for chronological classification: While retaining the traditional insignia colors, the Austro-Hungarian army had received a double-breasted tunic in 1849/50, which became single-breasted in 1859. From 1859 officers wore their sash over the right shoulder; from 1868 it was again worn around the waist. In 1868 the blue tunic with light blue or gray pants was ordered; under the influence of increasingly precise hand-held firearms (Zündnadel-Gewehr) during the first and second German unification wars (1864 and 1866), the typical white base color of the imperial uniforms had finally proven to be inappropriate (the pike-gray army uniform was issued in 1909). All parts of the so-called man's armor, also introduced in 1868 - waist belt, knapsack carrying frame and two cartridge pouches made of black dyed leather - were now exchanged for pieces made of brown upper leather in accordance with the "1881 pattern". In 1850, the existing cuirassier and chevauleger regiments were converted into dragoon and Uhlan units, all of which wore light blue skirts and madder red pants between 1868 and 1914 (the lances of the Uhlans had been without a flag since 1866; hussars wore dark blue dolman coats and furs with yellow cords).

PLATE 1

1. General-Adjutant (Parade) - 2. Flügel-Adjutant des Kaisers - 3. General-Artillerie-Inspector - 4. General-Genie-Inspector - 5. General in German Uniform (Gala) - 6. Generalstabs-Offizier (Parade) - 7. General in Hungarian Uniform (Gala) - 8. General-Auditor (Parade) - 9. General-Intendant (Parade) - 10. General medical staff - 11. General in German Uniform (Dienst) - 12. General in Hungarian Uniform (Service)

PLATE 2

1. K. K. Trabanten-Leibgarde (Gala) - 2. K. K. Trabanten-Leibgarde (ordinary unif.) - 3. K. K. Leibgarde-Inf.-Comp. (cloak) - 4. First Arcieren-Leibgarde (Gala) - 5. First Arcieren-Leibgarde (cloak) - 6. Leibgarde-Reiter-Eskadr. (gewöhnl. Unif.) - 7. Leibgarde-Inf.-Comp. (Gala) - 8. Hungarian Leibgarde (ordinary Unif.) - 9. Hungarian Crown Guard (Gala) - 10. Life Guards Rider Escadr. (Gala) - 11. Hungarian Life Guards Life Guards (Gala)

1., General-Adjutant (Parade.) — 2., Flügel-Adjutant des Kaisers. — 3., General-Artillerie-Inspector. — 4., General-Genie-Inspector. — 5., General in deutscher Uniform (Gala.) — 6., Generalstabs-Offizier (Parade.) — 7., General in ungar. Uniform (Gala.) — 8., General-Auditor (Parade.) — 9., General-Intendant (Parade.) — 10., General-Stabs-Arzt. — 11., General in deutscher Uniform (Dienst.) — 12., General in ungar. Uniform (Dienst.)

1., K. K. Trabanten-Leibgarde (Gala.) — 2., K. K. Trabanten-Leibgarde (Gewöhnl. Unif.) — 3., K. K. Leibgarde-Inf. Comp. (Mantel.) — 4., Erste Arcieren-Leibgarde (Gala.) — 5., Erste Arcieren-Leibgarde (Mantel.) — 6., Leibgarde-Reiter-Eskadr. (gewöhnl. Unif.) — 7., Leibgarde-Inf.-Comp. (Gala.) — 8., Ungar. Leibgarde (gewöhnl. Unif.) — 9., Ungar. Kronwache (Gala.) — 10., Leibgarde-Reiter-Eskadr. (Gala.) — 11., Ungar. Leib-Garde (Gala.)

"DIE OESTERREICH.-UNGARISCHE ARMEE" (VOR 1881/82) VERLAG MORITZ RUHL

PLATE 3

1. German Infantry in Parade-Unif. (11th Inf.-Reg.) - 2. Hungar. Infantry in overcoat (16th Inf.-Reg.) - 3. German Infantry, fielded (4th Inf.-Reg.) - 4. Hungarian Inf. Infant. in parade unif. (67th Inf.-Reg.) - 5. Kapellmeister (81st Inf.-Reg.) - 6. Infant. officer in blouse (64th Inf.-Reg.) - 7. Inf. officer in coat (94th Inf.-Reg.) - 8. Jäger officer in blouse - 9. Jäger, field-wise. - 10. Jäger in parade unif. - 11. Inf. officer in parade uniform. (26th Hungarian Inf. Reg.) - 12. Jäger officer in parade unif.

PLATE 4

1. 15th Dragoon Regiment - 2. Officer of 9th Dragoon Regiment (Parade) - 3. Officer of 3rd Dragoon Regiment - 4. Officer of 1st Hussar Regiment Reg. - 5. Officer of 14th Hussar Reg. - 6. Officer of 1st Uhlan Reg. - 7. Non-Commissioned Officer of 3rd Uhlan Reg. - 8. Non-Commissioned Officer of 7th Uhlan Reg. - 9. Coursmith of Cavalry - 10. 7th Drag. Reg. (Coat) - 11. 13. Drag.-Reg. (Parade) - 12. 11. Husaren-Reg. (field) - 13. 4. Uhlanen-Reg.

1., Deutsche Infant. in Parade-Unif. (11. Inf.-Reg.) — 2., Ungar. Infant. im Mantel (16. Inf.-Reg.) — 3., Deutsche Infant., feldmässig (4. Inf.-Reg.) — 4., Ungar. Infant. in Parade-Unif. (6. Inf.-Reg.) — 5., Kapellmeister (81. Inf.-Reg.) — 6., Infant.-Offizier in Blouse (64. Inf.-Reg.) — 7., Inf.-Offizier in Mantel (94. Inf.-Reg.) — 8., Jäger-Offizier in Blouse. — 9., Jäger, feldmässig. — 10., Jäger in Parade-Unif. — 11., Inf.-Offizier in Parade-Unif. (26. ungar. Inf.-Reg.) — 12., Jäger-Offizier in Parade-Unif.

1., 15. Dragoner-Reg. — 2., Offizier v. 9. Drag.-Reg. (Parade). — 3., Offizier v. 3. Drag.-Reg. — 4., Offizier v. 1. Husaren-Reg. — 5., Offizier vom 14. Husaren-Reg. — 6., Offizier vom 1. Uhlanen-Reg. — 7., Unteroff. v. 3. Uhlanen-Reg. — 8., Unteroff. v. 7. Uhlanen-Reg. — 9., Kurschmied v. d. Cavallerie. — 10., 7. Drag.-Reg. (Mantel.) — 11., 13. Drag.-Reg. (Parade). — 12., 11. Husaren-Reg. (feldmässig.) — 13., 4. Uhlanen-Reg.

"DIE OESTERREICH.-UNGARISCHE ARMEE" (VOR 1881/82) VERLAG MORITZ RUHL

PLATE 5

1. Field Artillery (regular dress) - 2. Fortress Artillery (parade) - 3. Technical Artillery (in greatcoat) - 4. Field Artillery Course Officer - 5. Field Artillery Non-Commissioned Officer (parade) - 6. Technical Artillery Officer (parade) - 7. Train Officer (in greatcoat) - 8. Technical Artillery - 9. Mountain Train - 10. Train (regular dress) - 11. Train Officer (parade) - 13. Fortress Artillery Officer - 13. Field Artillery Officer (parade) - 14. Train Non-Commissioned Officer (parade)

PLATE 6

1. Engineer Soldier (Service Unit) - 2. Engineer Soldier (Parade Unit) - 3. Engineer Officer (Service Unit) - 4. Engineer Staff Officer - 5. Pioneer Officer (Parade Unit) - 6. Pioneer - 7. Pioneer (Service Unit) - 8. Officer of the Iron Regiment - 9. Soldier of the Iron Regiment (Service Unit) - 10. Soldier of the Iron Regiment (Parade Unit) - 11. Engineer Officer (Parade Unit) - 12. Officer of the Iron Regiment (Parade Unit) - 13. Pioneer Officer (Service Unit)

1., Feld-Artillerie (gewöhnl. Anzug.) — 2., Festungs-Artillerie (Parade.) — 3., Techn. Artillerie [im Mantel.] — 4., Kurschmied d. Feld-Artillerie. — 5., Unteroff. d. Feld-Artillerie (Parade.) — 6., Offiz. d. techn. Artillerie (Parade.) — 7., Train-Offizier [im Mantel.] — 8., Techn. Artillerie. — 9., Gebirgs-Train. — 10., Train [gewöhnl. Anzug.] 11., Train-Offizier [Parade.] — 12., Offiz. der Festungs-Art. — 13., Offiz. der Feld-Art. [Parade.] — 14., Train-Unteroff. [Parade.]

1., Genie-Soldat (Dienst-Unif.) — 2., Genie-Soldat [Parade-Unif.] — 3., Genie-Offizier [Dienst-Unif.] — 4., Offizier v. Geniestab. — 5., Pionier-Offizier [Parade-Unif.] — 6., Pionier. — 7., Pionier [Dienst-Unif.] — 8., Offiz. v. Eisenb.-Reg. — 9., Soldat v. Eisenb.-Reg. (Dienst-Unif.) — 10., Soldat v. Eisenb.-Reg. [Parade-Unif.] — 11., Genie-Offiz. [Parade-Unif.] — 12., Offiz. v. Eisenb.-Reg. [Parade-Unif.] — 13., Pionier-Offizier [Dienst-Unif.]

"DIE OESTERREICH.-UNGARISCHE ARMEE" (VOR 1881/82) VERLAG MORITZ RUHL

PLATE 7

1. Medical soldier (field service) - 2. Officer of the medical corps (service uniform) - 3. Officer of the medical corps (parade uniform) - 4. Military doctor (parade uniform) - 5. Doctor (field service) - 6. Troop accountant (regular uniform) - 7. Troop accountant (parade uniform) - 8. Officer of the uniform branch (parade uniform) - 9. Non-commissioned officer of the uniform branch - 10. Military doctor (regular uniform) - 11. Officer of the veterinary institute (parade) - 12. Non-commissioned officer of the veterinary institute

PLATE 8

1. Intendant's Officer (in Blouse) - 2. Auditor - 3. Accounting, Catering, etc. Officer - 4. and 5. Officials of the Military-Geographical Institute - 6. Technical Officer of the Artillery Equipment Department - 7. Official of the Technical-Administrative Military Committees - 8. Veterinarian (Parade Unit) - 9. Veterinarian (Service Unit) - 10. Military Forestry Officer - 11. Pharmacist's Assistant - 12. Corporal of the Stallion Depot - 13. Officer of the Stallion Depot

1., Sanitäts-Soldat (feldmässig.) — 2., Offiz. der Sanitätstruppe (Dienst-Unif.) — 3., Offiz. der Sanitätstruppe (Parade-Unif.) — 4., Milit.-Arzt (Parade-Unif.) — 5., Arzt-Eleve (feldmässig.) — 6., Truppen-Rechnungsführer (gewöhnl. Unif.) — 7., Truppen-Rechnungsführer (Parade-Unif.) — 8., Offiz. d. Montur-Branche (Parade-Unif.) — 9., Unteroff. der Montur-Branche. — 10., Milit.-Arzt (gewöhnl. Anzug.) — 11., Offiz. v. Thierarznei-Inst. (Parade.) — 12., Unteroff. v. Thierarznei-Inst.

1., Intendanturs-Beamter (in Blouse.) — 2., Auditor. — 3., Rechnungs-, Verpflegs- etc. Beamter. — 4. u. 5., Beamte des mil.-geogr. Instituts. — 6., Techn. Beamter des Art.-Zeugwesens. — 7., Beamter der techn.-adm. Mil.-Comités. — 8., Thierarzt (Parade-Unif.) — 9., Thierarzt (Dienst-Unif.) — 10., Milit.-Forstbeamter. — 11., Apotheker-Gehilfe. — 12., Unteroff. v. Hengsten-Depot. — 13., Offizier v. Hengsten-Depot.

"DIE OESTERREICH.-UNGARISCHE ARMEE" (VOR 1881/82) VERLAG MORITZ RUHL

PLATE 9

1. Gunsmith 2nd Class (field) - 2. Food Service (Master 2nd Class) - 3. Foreman 1st Class - 4. Building Master 1st Class - 5. Sergeant - 6. Army Officer (Parade Unit) - 7. Retired Officer (91st Infantry Regiment) - 8. Officer of the Invalid Corps - 9. Invalid Corps (Soldier) - 10. Officer's Boy (Infantry) - 11. Hungarian Horse Breeder (NCO) - 12. Hungarian Horse Breeder (Officer in Parade Unit) - 13. Officer's Boy (Cavity)

PLATE 10

1. Cadet of the Infantry - 2. Cadet of the Artillery - 3. Cadet of the Pioneers - 4. Riding Instructor Assistant of the Technical Military Academy - 5. Training Non-Commissioned Officer - 6. Training Sergeant - 7. High School - 8. Lower School - 9. Military Academy - 10. Military Orphanage - 11. Bugler of the Military Educational Institution - 12. House Servant of the Military Educational Institution - 13. Cadet of the Cavalry - 14. Riding Instructor Assistant of the Riding Instructor Institute

1., Büchsenmacher 2. Kl. (feldmässig.) — 2., Verpflegungs-Branche (Meister 2. Kl.) — 3., Werkmeister 1. Kl. — 4., Bauwerkmeister 1. Kl. — 5., Profoss. — 6., Offizier des Armeestandes (Parade-Unif.) — 7., Offizier des Ruhestandes (91. Inf.-Reg.) — 8., Offizier v. Invalidencorps. — 9., Invalidencorps (Soldat.) — 10., Offiziersbursche (Infant.) — 11., Ungar. Pferdezucht-Anst. (Unteroff.) — 12., Ungar. Pferdezucht-Anst. (Offiz. in Parade-Unif.) — 13., Offiziersbursche (Cav.)

1., Cadett der Inf. — 2., Cadett der Art. — 3., Cadett der Pioniere. — 4., Reitlehrer-Gehilfe v. d. techn. Mil.-Akad. — 5., Lehr-Unteroffizier. — 6., Lehr-Feldwebel. — 7., Ober-Realschule. — 8., Unter-Realschule. — 9., Mil.-Akademie. — 10., Milit.-Waisenhaus. — 11., Hornist der Mil.-Bildungsanst. — 12., Haustiener d. Mil.-Bildungsanst. — 13., Cadett der Cav. — 14., Reitlehrer-Gehilfe v. Reitlehrer-Inst.

"DIE OESTERREICH.-UNGARISCHE ARMEE" (VOR 1881/82) VERLAG MORITZ RUHL

PLATE 11

1. Landwehr Infantry (field uniform) - 2. Landwehr Infantry (in greatcoat) - 3. Landwehr Infantry Officer (parade uniform) - 4. Landwehr Infantry Officer (field uniform) - 5. Agricultural District Sergeant - 6. Landwehr Cadet (in blouse) - 7. and 8. Regional Rifle Officers (in greatcoat and parade uniform) - 9. Agricultural Equipment Depot - 10. Regional Rifleman (field uniform) - 11. Tyrolean Regional Rifleman on horseback - 12. Officer of the Tyrolean Regional Riflemen on horseback (parade uniform) - 13. Officer of the mounted Regional Riflemen in Dalmatia - 14. Trumpeter of the mounted Regional Riflemen in Dalmatia

PLATE 12

1. Landwehr Doctor - 2. Landwehr Intendant - 3. Landwehr Technical Officer - 4. Landwehr Accounting Officer - 5. Landwehr Course Officer - 6. Landwehr Dragoon Officer (Parade Unit) - 7. Landwehr Squadron Strap Maker - 8. Landwehr Gunsmith - 9. Landsturm - 10. Tyrolean Landsturm - 11. Landwehr Uhlan Officer (Parade Unit) - 12. Landwehr Uhlan - 13. Landwehr Dragoon

1., **Landwehr-Inf. (feldmässig.)** — 2., **Landwehr-Inf. (im Mantel.)** — 3., **Landwehr-Inf.-Offizier (Parade-Unif.)** — 4., **Landwehr-Inf.-Off. (feldmässig.)** — 5., **Landw.-Bezirks-Feldwebel.** — 6., **Landwehr-Cadett (in Blouse.)** — 7. u. 8., **Landesschützen-Offiziere (im Mantel und in Parade-Unif.)** — 9., **Landw.-Ausrüstungs-Depot.** — 10., **Landesschütze (feldmässig.)** — 11., **Tirol. Landesschütze zu Pferd.** — 12., **Offiz. d. Tiroler Landesschützen z. Pferd (Parade-Unif.)** — 13., **Offiz. d. beritt. Landesschützen in Dalmatien.** — 14., **Trompeter d. beritt. Landesschützen in Dalmatien.**

1., **Landwehr-Arzt.** — 2., **Landw.-Intend.-Beamter.** — 3., **Techn. Beamter d. Landwehr.** — 4., **Rechnungsbeamter d. Landw.** — 5., **Kurschmied d. Landw.** — 6., **Landw.-Dragoner-Off. (Parade-Unif.)** — 7., **Eskadr.-Riemer d. Landw.** — 8., **Büchsenmacher d. Landw.** — 9., **Landsturm.** — 10., **Tiroler Landsturm.** — 11., **Landw.-Uhlanen-Off. (Parade-Unif.)** — 12., **Landw.-Uhlan.** — 13., **Landw.-Dragoner.**

"DIE OESTERREICH.-UNGARISCHE ARMEE" (VOR 1881/82) VERLAG MORITZ RUHL

PLATE 13

1. Honved Infantry Officer (in Blouse) - 2. Honved Infantry Officer (Parade Unit) - 3. Honved Infantry (Parade Unit) - 4. Honved District Sergeant (Parade Unit) - 5. Honved Infantry (in Coat) - 6. Honved Infantry (Field Uniform) - 7. Honved Hussar Officer (Ordinary Unit) - 8. Honved District Sergeant (Ordinary Unit) - 9. Ludovica Academy - 10. Honved Hussar (5th Regiment) - 11. Honved Hussar Officer (8th Regiment) - 12. Honved Hussar, Parade Unit (10th Regiment)

PLATE 14

1. Honved Accountant - 2. Honved Intendant's Office Official (Parade Uniform) - 3. and 4. Honved Auditor (in Blouse and in Parade Uniform) - 5. Honved Physician (Parade Uniform) - 6. Honved Veterinarian (Parade Uniform) - 7. and 8. Honved Gunsmith (in Parade Uniform and in Blouse) - 9. Hungarian Home Guard - 10. Honved Physician (in Blouse) - 11. Honved Cavalry School - 12. Honved Veterinarian (in Blouse)

1., Honved-Inf.-Off. (in Blouse.) — 2., Honved-Inf.-Off.(Parade-Unif.) — 3., Honved-Inf. (Parade-Unif.) — 4., Honved-Bezirks-Feldwebel (Parade-Unif.) — 5., Honved-Inf. (im Mantel.) — 6., Honved-Inf. (feldmässig.) — 7., Honved-Husaren-Off. (gewöhnl. Unif.) — 8., Honved-Bezirks-Feldwebel (gewöhnl. Unif.) — 9., Ludovica-Akad. — 10., Honved-Husar (5. Reg.) — 11., Honved-Husaren-Off. (8. Reg.) — 12., Honved-Husar, Parade-Unif. (10. Reg.)

1., Honved-Rechnungsbeamter. — 2., Honved-Intendantur-Beamter (Parade-Unif.) — 3. u. 4., Honved-Auditor (in Blouse u. in Parade-Unif.) — 5., Honved-Arzt (Parade-Unif.) — 6., Honved-Thierarzt (Parade-Unif.) — 7. u. 8., Honved-Büchsenmacher (in Parade-Unif. u. in Blouse.) — 9., Ungar. Landsturm. — 10., Honved-Arzt (in Blouse.) — 11., Honved-Cav.-Schule. — 12., Honved-Thierarzt (in Blouse.)

"DIE OESTERREICH.-UNGARISCHE ARMEE" (VOR 1881/82) VERLAG MORITZ RUHL

PLATE 15

1. Corporal of the Bosnian Infantry - 2. Bosnian Infantry - 3. Officer of the Bosnian Infantry - 4. Bosnian Gendarme (Muslim) - 5. Bosnian Military Boys' Boarding School - 6. Bosnian Gendarme (Christian) - 7. and 8. Imperial and Royal State Gendarmes (in cap and parade uniform) - 9. Guard Corps for Civil Courts - 10. Military Police Guard Corps - 11. Bosnian Train Soldier - 12. Officer of the Imperial and Royal State Gendarmerie (in blouse) - 13. Officer of the Hungarian Gendarmerie (in parade uniform) - 14. Hungarian Mounted Gendarme.

PLATE 16

1. Hydrographic Officer (Department Head) - 2. Technical Naval Officer (Engineer 1st Class) - 3. Naval Commissioner (Adjunct 3rd Class) - 4. Naval Staff Surgeon - 5. Frigate Captain (Grand Service Dress) - 6. Vice Admiral (Parade Uniform) - 7. Rear Admiral (Ordinary Dress) - 8. Lieutenant of the Line (in Parade Uniform) - 9. Sea Cadet 1st Class (Ordinary Dress) - 10. Chief Helmsman - 11. Sailor - 12. Boatswain's Mate (in white dress)

1., Unteroff. d. bosn. Inf. — 2., Bosnische Infanterie. — 3., Offizier d. bosn. Inf. — 4., Bosn. Gendarm (Muhamedaner.) — 5., Bosn. Milit.-Knaben-Pensionat. — 6., Bosn. Gendarm (Christ.) — 7. u. 8., K. K. Landes-Gendarmen (in Mütze u. in Parade-Unif.) — 9., Wachcorps für Civilgerichte. — 10., Milit.-Polizei-Wachcorps. — 11., Bosn. Train-Soldat. — 12., Off. d. K. K. Landes-Gendarmerie (in Blouse.) — 13., Off. d. ungar. Gendarmerie (in Parade-Unif.) — 14., Ungar. beritt. Gendarm.

1., Beamter d. hydrogr. Wesens (Abth.-Vorst.) — 2., Techn. Marine-Beamter (Ingenieur 1. Kl.) — 3., Marine-Komiss.-Beamter (Adjunkt 3. Kl.) — 4., Marine-Stabrarzt. 5., Fregatten-Kapitän (Gr. Dienstanzug.) — 6., Vice-Admiral (Parade-Unif.) — 7., Contre-Admiral (gewöhnl. Anzug.) — 8., Linienschiffslieutenant (in Parade-Unif.) 9., Seecadett 1. Kl. (gewöhnl. Anzug.) — 10., Obersteuermann. — 11., Matrose. — 12., Bootsmanns-Maat (in weissem Anzug.)

"DIE OESTERREICH-UNGARISCHE ARMEE" 1897-1898 J.V.KULAS

Illustrations of the K.u.K. army with artworks of the Austrian painter J.V.Kulas

Uniforms Plates:

Plate 1 Generals , major Staff
Plate 2 Leibgarden
Plate3 Health troops, auditor, chaplains
Plate 4 Infantry troops
Plate 5 Cavalry troops
Plate 6 Artillery and train
Plate 7 engineer troops, pioneers and telegraph
Plate 8 Landwher and Gendarmerie
Plate 9 Intendency and technical troops
Plate 10 Parade infantry soldiers and officers
Plate 11 Infantry weapons
Plate 12 High officer Ranks and badges

Marine Uniforms:

Plate 13 Navy uniforms
Plate 14 Navy standards and flags
Plate 15 sailor and NCO ranks and badges
Plate 16 Navy officers ranks and badges
Plate 17 Navy speciality badges

Plate 18 Flag and Standards of K.u.K.

Kavallerie.

Artillerie, Traintruppe, Gestütsbranche.

Intendanz, Truppen-Rechnungsführer, Militär-Beamte.

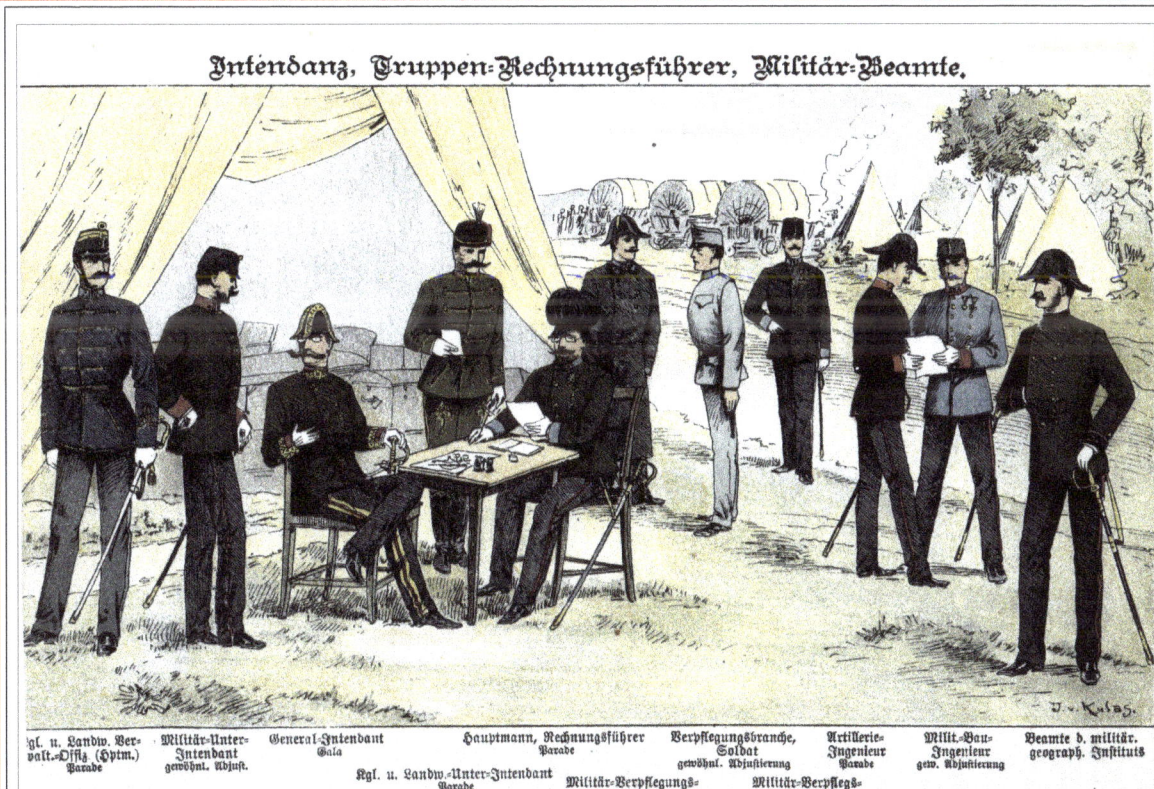

Kgl. u. Landw. Verwalt.-Offiz. (Hptm.) Parade — Militär-Unter-Intendant gewöhnl. Adjust. — General-Intendant Gala — Kgl. u. Landw.-Unter-Intendant Parade — Hauptmann, Rechnungsführer Parade — Militär-Verpflegungsbeamte Winterparade — Verpflegungsbranche, Soldat gewöhnl. Adjustierung — Militär-Verpflegs-Offizial gewöhnl. Adjust. — Artillerie-Ingenieur Parade — Milit.-Bau-Ingenieur gew. Adjustierung — Beamte d. militär. geograph. Instituts

In Paradeadjustierung:
1. Kaiserjäger, Jäger oder österr. Landwehr. — 2. Diensttuender Feldwebel, ungar. Reg. — 3. Bosnisch-herzegow. Jäger. — 4.–6. Infanterie, deutsche Reg. (4. Fahnenführer. — 5. Korporal. — 6. Oberleutnant.) — 7. Bosnisch-herzegow. Infanterist. — 8. Jäger- od. Landwehr-Stabsoffizier. — 9. Offizier d. Landesschützen od. d. Landwehr-Int.-Reg. Nr. 4. — 10. u. 11. Königl. ungar. Honvéd (10. Offizier. — 11. Infanterist).

Ausrüstungs-Gegenstände.

1, 2. Gewehre. 3, 4. Infanterie-Spaten. 5, 6. Bajonett. 7, 8. Pionier-Säbel. 9. Signalhorn. 10, 11. Infanterie-Säbel. 12. Leibriemen-Schloß. 13. Beilpicke. 14. Trommeltragriemen. 15. Beilpicke. 16. Feldflasche. 17. Tornister. 18. Trommel. 19. Tornister. 20, 21. Offiziers-Säbel.

Grad- und sonstige Abzeichen.

1. Feldmarschall. 2. Feldzeugmeister u. General d. K. 3. Feldmarschall-Leutnant. 4. General-Major. 5. Oberst. 6. Oberstleutnant. 7. Major. 8. Hauptmann u. Rittmeister. 9. Oberleut. 10. Leutnant. 11. Kadett-Offiziers-Stellvertreter. 12. Feldwebel. 13. Zugsführer. 14. Korporal. 15. Gefreiter. 16. Leutnant d. Eisenbahn- u. Telegraphen-Rgts. 17. Militär-Intendant. 18. M.-Verpflegs-Verwalter. 19. Accessist. 20. Kapellmeister. 21. Sanitäts-Armbinde. 22. Oberstabs-Wagenmeister. 23. Stabs-Wagenmeister. 24. Wagenmeister b. Regimenter. 25. Marketender. 26. Feldbinde. 27. Kavallerie-Schütz.-Abz. 28. Infanterie-Schützen-Abzeichen. 29. Feldbinde f. zugeteilten Generalstabsoffiziere. 30. Gürtel. 31. Unteroffiziers-Portepee. 32. Offiziers-Portepee. 33. Offiziers-Armlitze. 34. Mannschafts-Armlitze. 35. Pelz-Ärmelverzierung f. ungar. Generals-Uniform. 36. Attila-Ärmelverzierung f. ungar. Generals-Uniform.

Schiffsfähnrich Adjutant in gr. Dienstuniform | Offizier im Dienst Flaggen-Offizier | Seestabsoffizier | Generalkommissär | Matrose | Unteroffizier im Sommeranzug | Matrose im Mantel Oberbootsmann (daneben im Winteranzug) | Matrose in feldmäßiger Ausrü[stung]

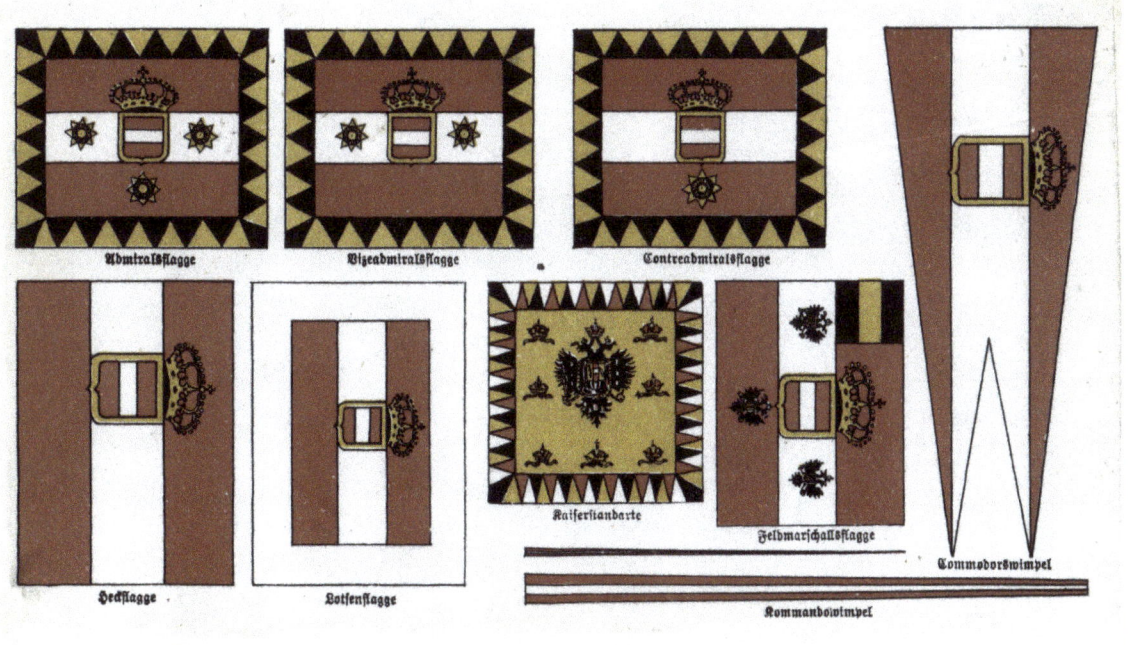

Admiralsflagge | Vizeadmiralsflagge | Contreadmiralsflagge | Heckflagge | Lotsenflagge | Kaiserstandarte | Feldmarschallflagge | Commodorswimpel | Kommandowimpel

Mannschafts-Abzeichen, Säbel, Kappen und Hüte.

1. Offiziersäbel. 2. Matrosen 2., 3. und 4. Klasse. 3. Matrose 1. Klasse. 4. Marsgast und Quartiermeister. 5. Bootsmannmaat. 6. Beamtensäbel. 7. Niedere Unteroffiziere (K... Unterbootsmann-, 9. Bootsmann-, 10. Oberbootsmanns-Armdistinktion. 11. Matrosenkappe. 12. Armstreifen nach 10 Jahren Dienstzeit. 13. Abzeichen des Einjährig-Freiwi... 14. Admiralshut. 15. Bootsmannskappe. 16. General-Kommissär. 17. Stabsoffizier. 18. Oberoffizier.

Offiziers- und Beamten-Abzeichen.

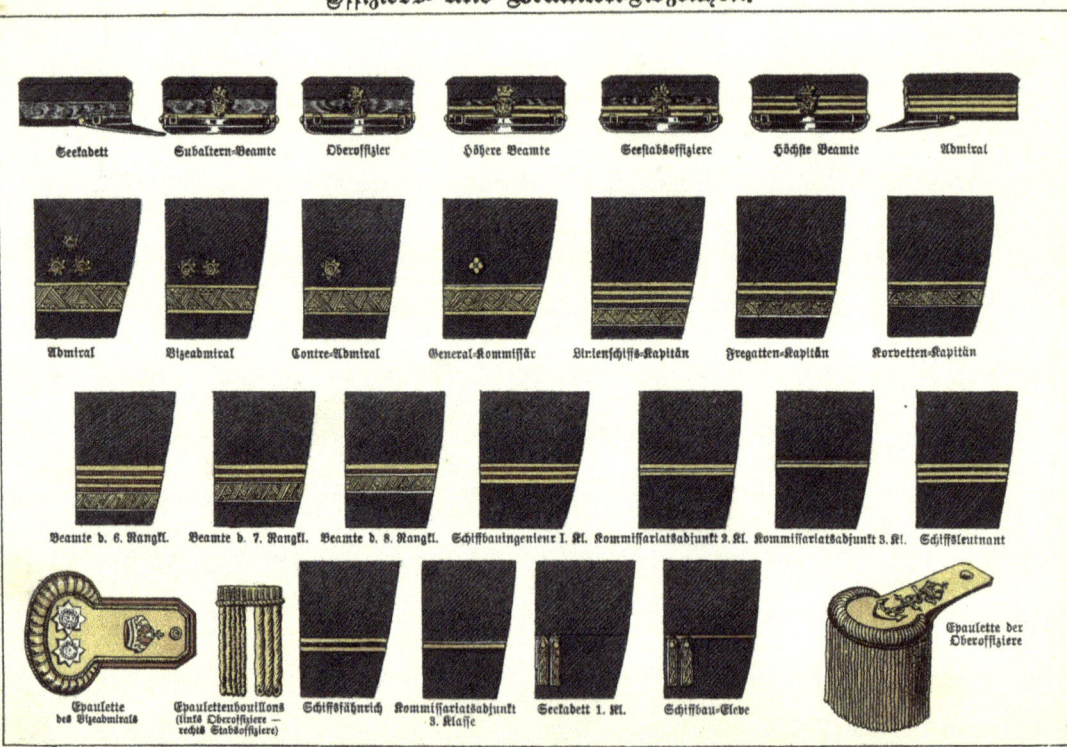

Seekadett. Subaltern-Beamte. Oberoffizier. Höhere Beamte. Seestabsoffiziere. Höchste Beamte. Admiral.

Admiral. Vizeadmiral. Contre-Admiral. General-Kommissär. Linienschiffs-Kapitän. Fregatten-Kapitän. Korvetten-Kapitän.

Beamte d. 6. Rangkl. Beamte d. 7. Rangkl. Beamte d. 8. Rangkl. Schiffbauingenieur I. Kl. Kommissariatsadjunkt 2. Kl. Kommissariatsadjunkt 3. Kl. Schiffsleutnant.

Epaulette des Vizeadmirals. Epaulettenbouillons (links Oberoffiziere — rechts Stabsoffiziere). Schiffsfähnrich. Kommissariatsadjunkt 3. Klasse. Seekadett 1. Kl. Schiffbau-Eleve. Epaulette der Oberoffiziere.

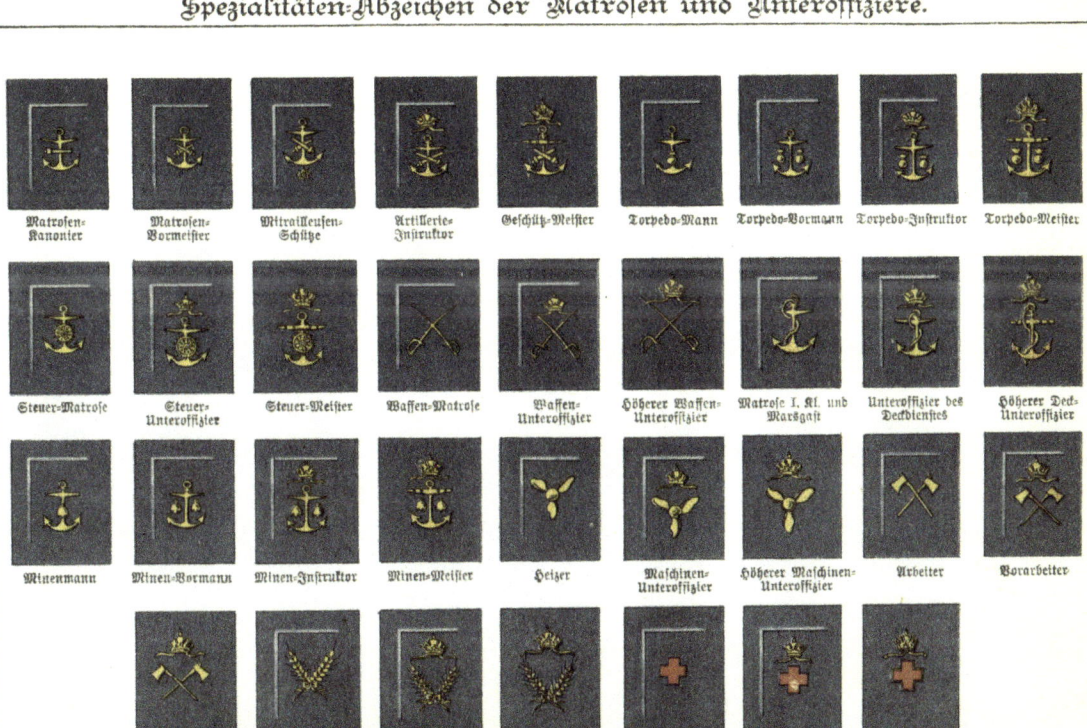

Spezialitäten-Abzeichen der Matrosen und Unteroffiziere.

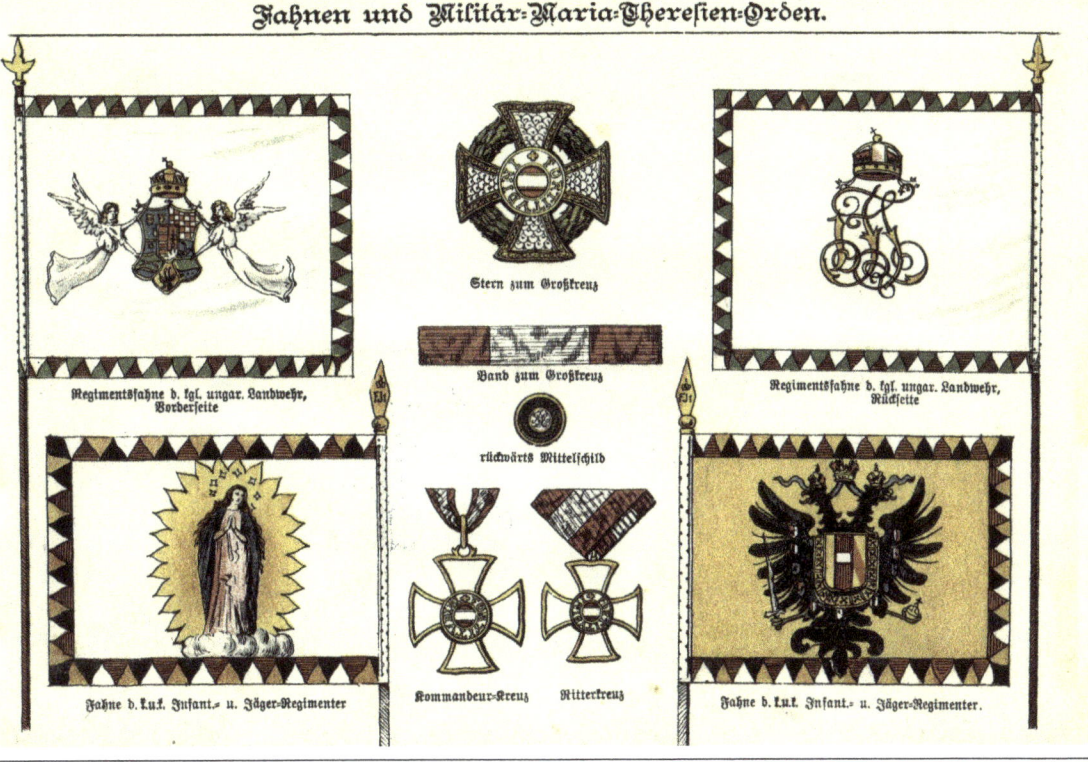

Fahnen und Militär-Maria-Theresien-Orden.

Die Adjustierung der Armee Oesterreich-Ungarns mit Berücksichtigung der bis zum Monate März 1877 erschienenen hohe Vorschriften in 22 Blätter.

A precious book of Illustrations of the K.u.K. army with drawings by K.K. Oberleutnant Friedrich Franceschini; With 22 lithographs and 2 supplements Edited by Verlags-Kunsthandlung S. Czeiger (ed.) : Vienna Publisher: Haupt & Czeiger

Our prints come from the collection of Dr Viskuezzen now owned by NYPL New York USA, whom we thank for their gracious permission to use them.

The plates themselves are often in a very poor state of preservation, so they have all undergone rigorous restoration by our technicians and graphic designers.

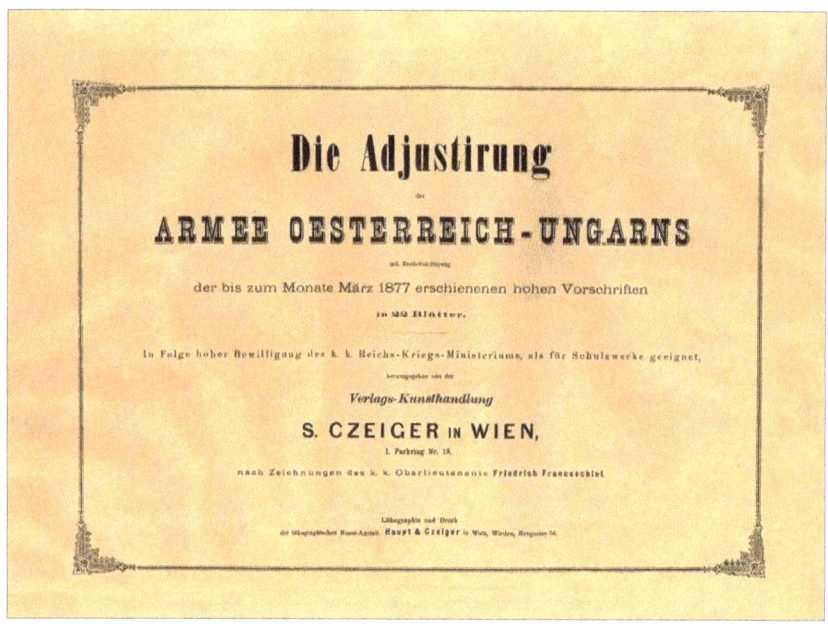

▲ Portrait of Sr. imperial Highness Archduke Leopold K.k. General of the Cavalry, General-Genie-Inspector; Sr. kaiserl. Highness Archduke Wilhelm K.k. Feldzeugmeister, General -Artillery-Inspect.
At right: Sr. kaiserl. Highness Crown Prince and heir to the throne Archduke Rudolf as Colonel-in-Chief of the 2nd Art. regiment; His Imperial and Royal Majesty Franz Josef I

▲ Portrait of Sr. kais. Highness Archduke Albrecht, K.k. Field Marshal, General-Inspect. of the k.k. Army; Sr. kais. Highness Archduke Josef, K.k. General of Cavalry, Commander-in-Chief of the Territorial Army of the Lands of the Hungarian Crown. Crown; Sr. kais. Highness Archduke Rainer

▲ Portrait of Byland-Rheidt Gr. K.k. Field Marshal Lieut. Reichs-Kriegs-Minister (German general's uniform) on parade; Schönfeld Fhr. K.k. Feldmschal Lieut. Chief of the Imperial-Royal. General Staff (in gala uniform). At Right: Pejacsevich v. Veröcze General of Cavalry. Cavalry-Inspector (Hungarian general's uniform), on parade; K.k. Oberlieutenant assigned to the k.k. General Staff

▲ K.k. Captain in the k.k. General Staff Corps (on parade); Field Adjutants of His Majesty the Emperor and King and officers employed in His Majesty's Military Chancellery (on parade)

▲ Captain-Auditor. (in Parade); General-Auditor (Gala). General-Intendant.

▲ Mil. clergy (on parade); retired officer (on parade); staff officer and NCO of the invalid supply rank

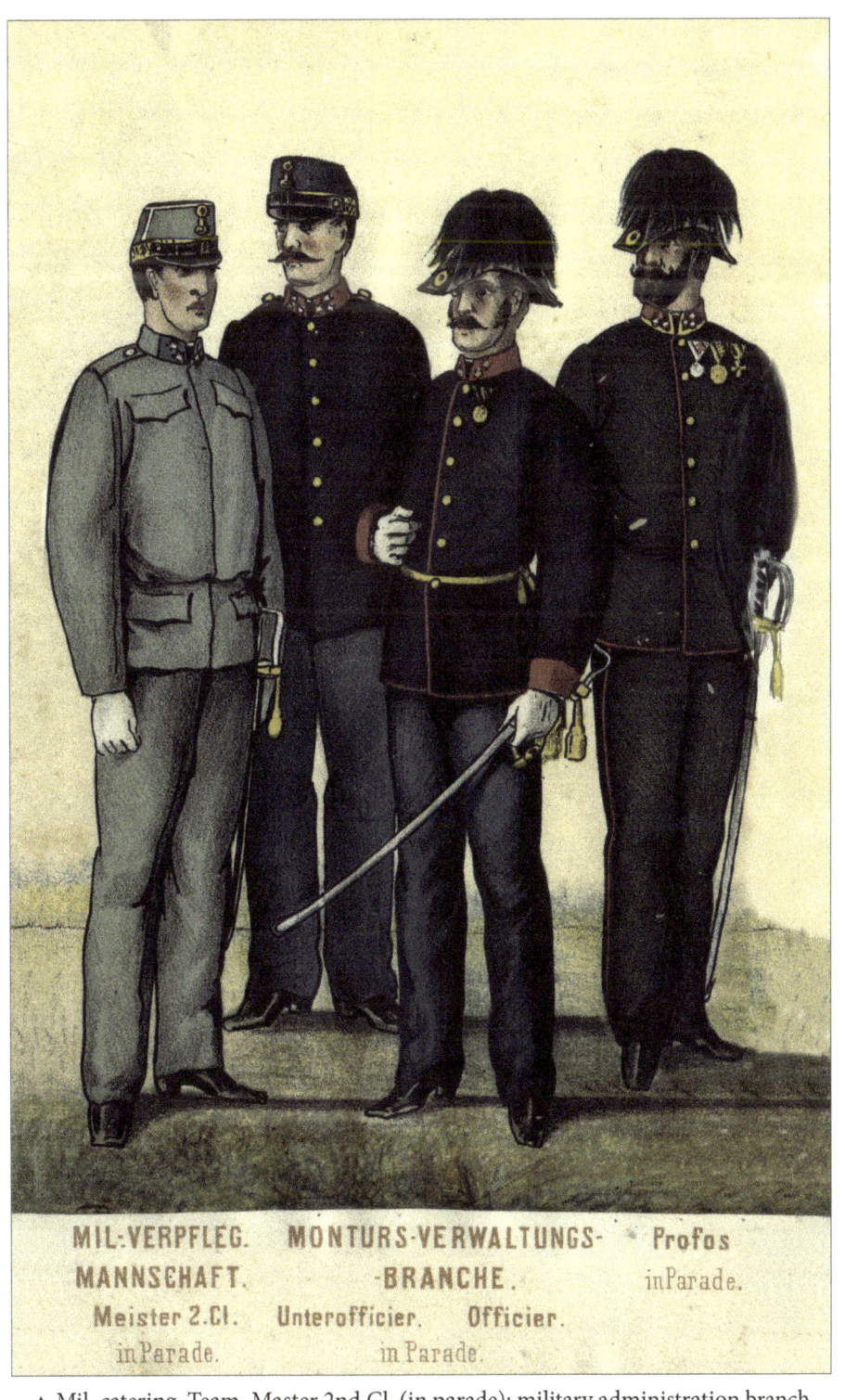

▲ Mil. catering. Team. Master 2nd Cl. (in parade); military administration branch NCO, Officer (in parade); Profos (in parade)

▲ Artillery gunner (on parade), artilleryman (field), NCO of the fortress art. (on parade), Officier der technisch. Artilleryman (on parade), staff officer of the field artillery

▲ Officer, battery trumpeter of the field artillery (on parade)

▲ Mil.Thier-Arztnei-Institut [from left to right], Staff Officer (in Parade), Soldat, NCO (in Parade), Ober-Their-Arzt (in Parade), Curschmid (on parade)

▲ Technical Auxiliary Personnel Master (in parade), at right: Medical unit soldier (field), NCO and officer

▲ Hussars Officer (field), Hussar (field), NCO (on parade), Officer (on parade)

▲ Hussars Officer in parade

▲ Cavalry uniforms: NCO (parade); officer (Sommer Attile and trousers; Stalladjustrg.)

▲ Cavalry uniforms: Honved Uhlanen Officier (parade with coat); Ober-Arzt, Auditor (parade)

▲ Infantry uniforms: Drummer, NCO and Officers in parade dress

▲ Infantry uniforms: Privates soldiers and NCO

▲ Jäger Officier (in Parade), NCO (in Parade), Cadet and Patrouilleführer (feldmässig)

▲ Infantry uniform of private and Nco. At right: litary chaplain, health service adept and doctor

KÖNG. UNG. HONVED-ARMEE

Stabsfeldwebel — Büchsenmacher — Mil. Rechnungs-Beamte — Militär-Intendantur-Beamte / Milit. Unter-Intendant I. Cl. — Köng. ungr. Kronwache Garde — Officier

K.k. Truppen Rech-nungsführer — K.k. Uhlanen Unterofficier / Officier — K.k. Genie Stab Adjutant Hauptmann / Ordonanz Officier — K.k. Leibgarde Reiter Escadron — K.k. Landes-Gendarmerie Officier / Unterofficier

K.K. LANDWEHR

SR MAJEST. KRIEGS-MARINE

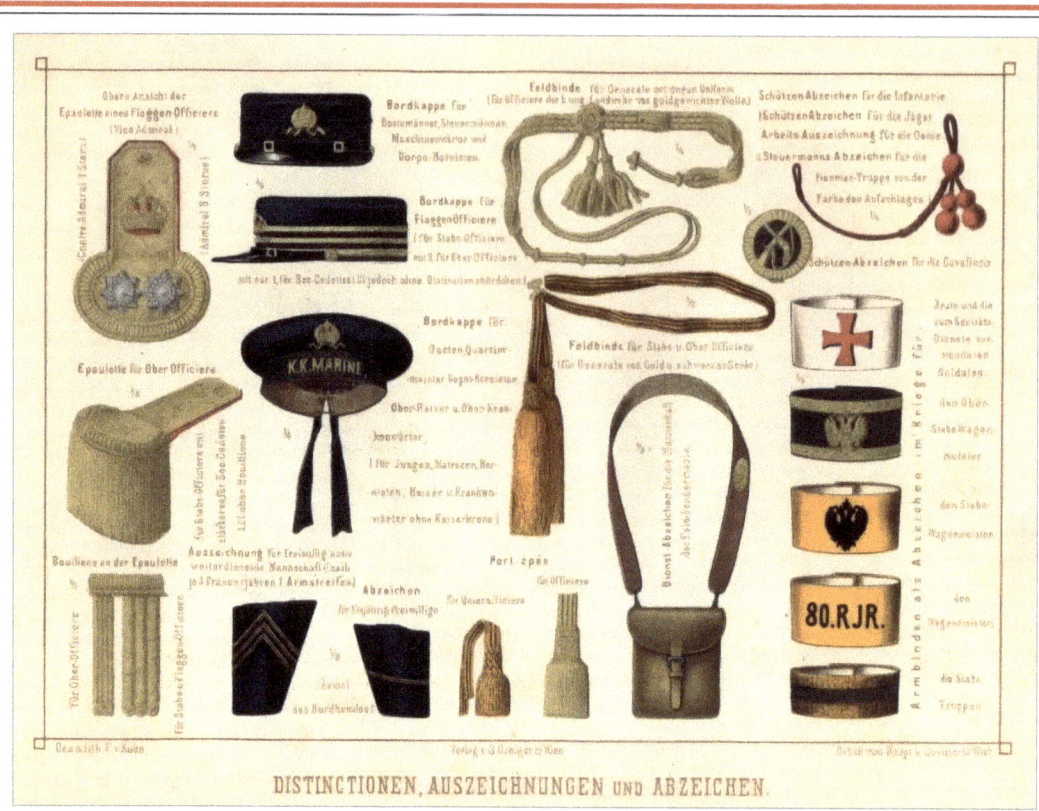

DISTINCTIONEN, AUSZEICHNUNGEN UND ABZEICHEN.

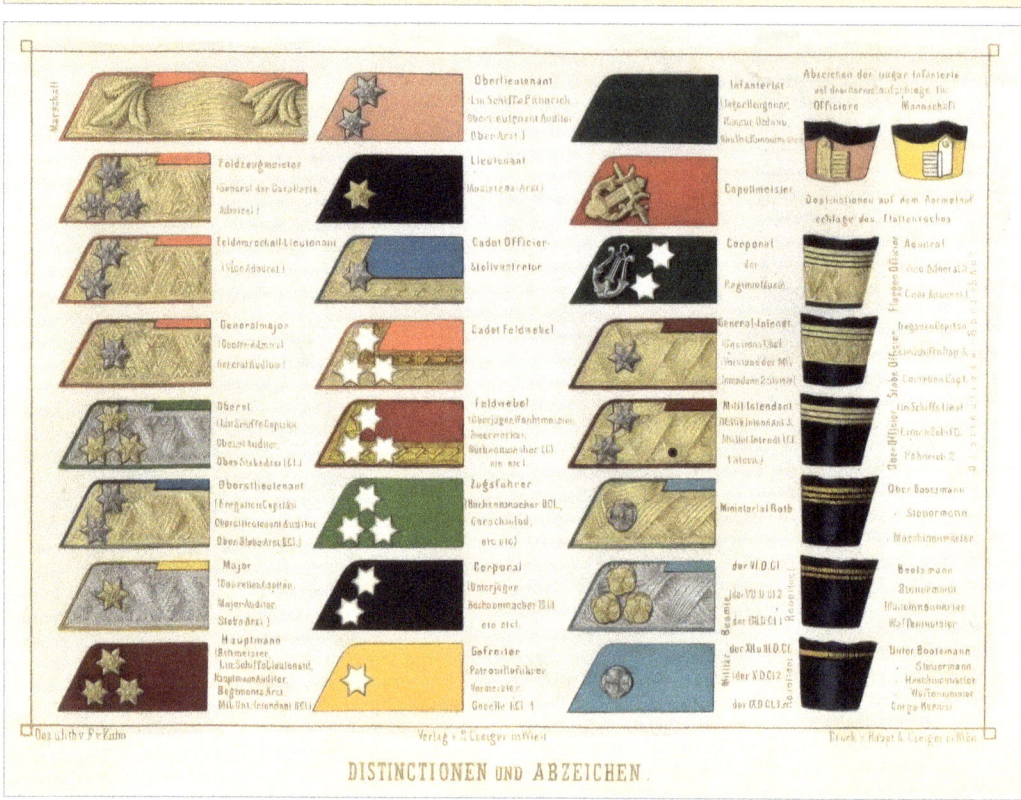

DISTINCTIONEN UND ABZEICHEN.

▲ Portrait of Kaiser Franz Joseph in 1865. By Franz Xaver Winterhalter Kunsthistorisches Museum Vienna Austria.

CONTENTS

Preface pag. 7

★

First Section
The Uniforms Distinctive and Other Insignia of the
Austro-Hungarian Imperial Army 1880   Pag.7

Seconda sezione.
Compagnie delle Reali Guardie del Corpo Pag. 32

First Section Plates
Corpo della Guardia d'Onore Pag. 55

Second Section
Appendix
Plates of the work of J.V.Kulas, Frederich Franceschini, Moritz Ruhl Pag. 89

First Part
"Die oesterreich.-ungarische Armee" 1880 Verlag Moritz Ruhl Pag. 90

Second Part
"Die Oesterreich-Ungarische Armee" 1897-1898 J.V.Kulas Pag. 106

Third part
"Die adjustirung der armee Oesterreich-Ungarns" F.Franceschini 1877-1884 Pag. 116

SOLDIERS, WEAPONS & UNIFORMS ALREADY PUBLISHED
(SOME TITLES)

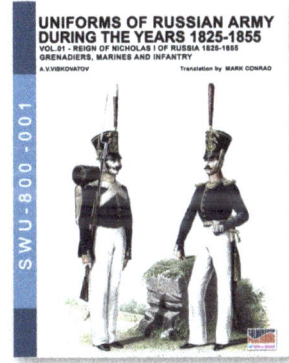
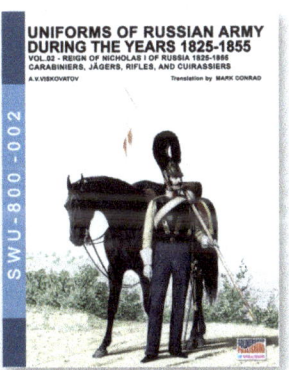

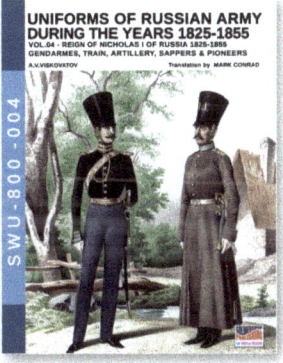

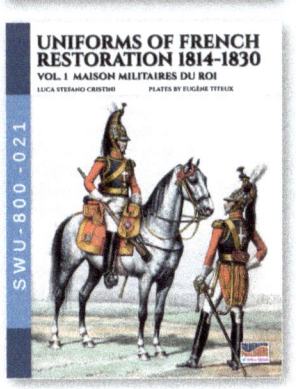
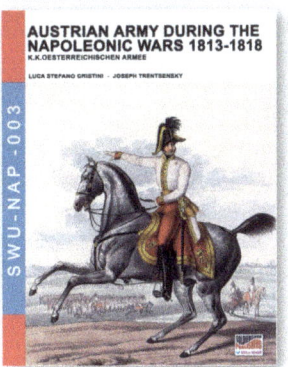
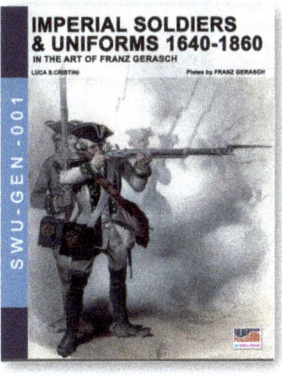

www.ingramcontent.com/pod-product-compliance
Lightning Source LLC
LaVergne TN
LVHW070526070526
838199LV00073B/6712